STIRRUP STORIES and LAMBS' TALES

Country Days – and Nights – with Animals

by Anne Holland

Published by New Generation Publishing in 2022

First Edition

Paperback: 978-1-80369-363-7
Hardback: 978-1-80369-364-4
Ebook: 978-1-80369-365-1

www.newgeneration-publishing.com

New Generation Publishing

Contents

DEDICATION:

to Tim, Lesley and George – and in memory of T, too.

ACKNOWLEDGEMENTS:

First and foremost a huge thank you to Brough Scott for writing the foreword in his inimitable and succinct style.

Back in the day, Brough rode some hundred winners as an amateur and then professionally. Nowadays, he is best known as a TV racing presenter and pundit, and racing writer – he has written many column inches for newspapers –and award-winning author. In all, he has devoted some six decades to the sport.

Brough has been a Trustee of the Injured Jockeys Fund since 1978, was Chairman from 2007 to 2019 and is now a life-long Vice President. He was awarded the MBE in 2009 for Services to Sport. All of us in racing owe him a debt of gratitude.

Also, a heartfelt thank you to all those men, women, children, dogs, orphan lambs – and especially horses – who have made my life so rich and fulfilled.

Thanks also go to the known photographers, *Kent and Sussex Courier, Horse and Hound*, Bernard Parkin, Sarah-Jane Bullock *(front cover, top, and back cover)*, Jim Meads, Clive Osborne, Shutterstock *(front cover bottom), the late Margaret Holland, a number from family albums* – some of which show their age, apologies to their photographers, and, importantly, to those who so far, the author has been unable to ascertain.

Also, to Malcolm Fraser for the front cover design and the cartoons, to Jane Hannath for her drawings, and to my sister-in-law, Tessa Holland for her read through and sound advice.

Anne Holland

FOREWORD

This is the book we all say we are going to write but never do.

As the shadows lengthen we look back to days that will never come again and vow to write them down as witness for later generations. But we don't. We dither and delay until it all gets so complicated that the enthusiasm wanes, contemporaries pass on, and the whole project gets stuffed into that top drawer of the memory chest which is already spilling over.

But Anne Holland has done it. Even for those of us old enough to have them, the memories of fifty and sixty years ago are fading fast. Now she has brought her own all back. A distant, simpler, crazier, happier country world where the days could still welcome the cry of hounds and the sound of the horn; where the point-to-point was both a celebration of old tradition and a breakthrough space for women in sport.

Anne has opened the door. Step right in and enjoy the journey. She has earned not just our thanks, but that of history too.

Brough Scott
April 2022

STIRRUP STORIES and LAMBS' TALES

Country Days – and Nights – with Animals

by Anne Holland

Fools and the Flock

It was 200 wits pitted against two, a battle of nerves to be fought to the bitter end.

We tried desperately to herd the flock into the warmth and shelter of the old barn before darkness fell; obstinately they refused to come in from the cold, oblivious of our good intentions, wary of all things human. We stamped our feet and they stamped back, snorting short fiery breaths into the cold evening air. Frantically we swung our arms like windmills in a gale accompanied by high-pitched vocal encouragement; a passer-by might have thought a murderer was inflicting mortal pain. But there was no-one besides the two of us and the 200 of them on that sparkling frosty night in April when it felt more like the Scottish Highlands than the Sussex Weald, with patches of snow still lying in sheltered nooks. They stood stock still, at stalemate, refusing to budge, only a few feet away from the barn entrance.

'Does anyone know the tune to "We shall not be moved?"'

We had coaxed the sheep that far quite easily really. Determined that they should not lamb out in such weather, we conned the ewes into thinking it was feeding time. T stood at the gate rattling the plastic bag they associated with corn, and I ran round the perimeter of the undulating field, chivvying the stragglers along the bottom, whooping wildly.

Just as I slowed to a walk, warm now that my blood was running, one ewe flashed by. Surprising how nimble a heavily pregnant Romney ewe can be. Back I went for the errant beast while T led the rest down the track towards the barn, shaking the bag to encourage them. They trotted along behind, à la Pied Piper.

And there we stood, T in front, me behind the bunched-up ewes. All they had to do was take the one remaining route, into the barn. Try telling them that!

'We need a sheep dog!' It was not the last time that heartfelt cry was to be heard.

One ewe darted past me and jumped the ditch like a two-year-old filly with springs in her heels. As I ran after her, another bunched slipped out behind.

'Don't let them get away, shout at them' yelled T. I grabbed a stick and flurried it against a woolly backside. It only felt like a pat to her ladyship who returned a quizzical stare from beneath her forelock, champing her mouth indignantly at her thwarted escape.

At last, one ewe got bored with the 'game', sniffed the entrance to the barn, pointed her best foot forward and tripped in inquisitively. The rest, of course, followed like sheep…

When the ewes were crammed into the barn, we pulled the netting across the entrance, stood back and gazed at our tranquil flock.

At once it became apparent that they were far from peaceful. The air was thick with steam, the atmosphere clogged as 200 sheep stood panting and obviously far too hot, thanks to their heavy fleeces. Worse still, the underfoot conditions were atrocious. What had seemed a reasonable earthen floor beforehand was now a soggy, seeping quagmire as the sheep stomped around.

* * *

This was not how we thought it would be when we had dreamed those dreams, and found the cottage and farm in 1974. Nor had my early years indicated in any way that sheep farming might enter my life.

II

Pony Mad Tom-boy

Because it's there.

Exploring granny's garden, I discovered a strange object. It was in with the vegetables beyond the lawn. Behind was a high mellow brick wall with a pear tree against it and a number of soft fruit bushes beneath. But it was the contraption that caught my eye: it glistened in the sunshine and to my two-year-old self it represented Everest – or the Grand National. What would happen if I stamped on it?

A few moments later blood as red as the geraniums growing in the brightly coloured border was pouring as if from a jug just below my left knee, cut by the glass of what, I later learnt, was called a cold frame. I ran down the long, neatly mown lawn screaming; behind me my toddler sister, Patsy, was bawling because I was. The back door of the tall white-painted Victorian house was flung open and my normally non-athletic mother tore down the wrought iron-railed stone steps, and her frail mother, my elderly grandmother, followed, a vision indelibly ingrained in my memory.

They rushed me to the Kent and Sussex Hospital, Tunbridge Wells, and there I was placed on an ironing board (in truth, no doubt, an operating table). Four stitches were inserted in the wound to make the first of many physical scars, each with its own tale to tell. That one proved mighty useful at Mead School where I went at four. When learning my left from my right as we walked along in crocodile formation, I would kick my scarred leg into the air to check I'd got the right one (I mean left, of course).

Another time at two years old I got lost; I had wandered off up Montacute Road, down Frant Road and the steep hill that leads to the Pantiles round the bend at the bottom. It must have been mind-blowingly worrying for my mother and nanny, from whose care I'd doubtless toddled off, but all I remember is eating a gorgeous, gooey jam doughnut in the delicious smelling little corner bakery shop by the Pantiles, the Regency centre of fashion and spa water that made Tunbridge Wells famous in the 18th century. A number of years after my escapade an oil tanker went out of control down that hill, failed to negotiate the bend, and embedded itself in the corner house. The driver escaped unhurt and by an act of God or fate the little old lady inside had just gone out to the back to make a cup of tea.

From the age of four I nurtured two ambitions: to be a writer, like my mother, and to ride in a point-to-point. The first was always a part of me, I loved nothing more than writing stories at school. The second would have to wait – 'over my dead body does a daughter of mine race' was a familiar phrase from my father, Rex, while we were growing up. It didn't help that there were no horses in the family, let alone any horsey knowledge, but it was those regular spring outings to the local point-to-points that fired my imagination, stimulating my unswerving passion. One day I would be out there, wearing the silks, soaring over the fences – and winning. As it was, my sister and I had to make do with attending the races wearing the dark brown, wide-thighed jodhpurs and pretend jockey cap that were de rigueur for countless little girls back in the 1950s.

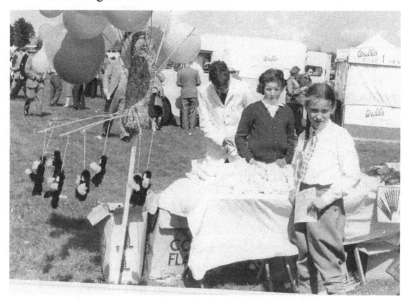

The author longed for nothing more than to point-to-point from an early age. 1950s fashion.

At the point-to-point, the parents perused the race-cards and discussed prospects. Would the pale blue with brown stars of Chris Nesfield's Steel Drop prevail again? Or would the chocolate and pink of Michael French's blinkered rogue Hymettus decide to put his best foot forward? John French might have a ride and his wife certainly would. Shelagh French began race-riding the year I was born, 1947, and was bound to be favourite for the ladies race. But then 'Miss Frightened Lady', the plump Pat Palmer came along with Canon Flame to win a good few; in later years she raced a number of her home-bred stallions. My 'career' was to overlap with both these redoubtable ladies. But in those young days I looked on in wonderment and awe – and tucked in to Nanny's delicious poppy seed bread and all sorts of salads, and Dad's favourite coffee date cake made by Nan.

Then, the parents were off to place their bets, either with a preferred bookmaker, or to walk up and down the line of bookies searching for the best price. Patsy and I would go to the paddock and look at the horses and jockeys, admiring their resplendent colours and making our choice. We would find the car amongst the rows of other similar black cars by the duster that was attached to its aerial. I would often go out into the infield and talk to a couple and their handsome black Labrador who I adored; the couple usually wore the cream riding macs of the era, smart and crisp-cut, unlike the wrinkly (and sometimes smelly) wax coats of today; their names escape me but the lovely dog was called Daniel.

One of the things we enjoyed most was after the last race when Patsy and I scoured the area that had held the bookmakers' stands. It was like being on a treasure hunt searching for the dropped coins, a tanner (sixpence – 2 ½ pence in 21st century money) here, a shilling there and, just occasionally, half-a-crown (2/6d; 12 ½ p): riches indeed. Mum and Dad would be entertaining friends at the car boot with, I think, more whiskey than wine. There was no breathalyser in those days (and far fewer cars on the roads) – indeed, another part of the day out was stopping at a pub on the way home, often the Star and Garter in Goudhurst, atop a steep hill, just below the church and its ancient yew trees; Patsy and I preferred that one because it was child-friendly.

There was a point-to-point at Ightham, Kent, a pretty course of an outer circuit taken twice and an inner circuit; the last bend was beside a large oak tree, invariably just coming into leaf, and riders had to beware its roots; it was a course to suit a handy horse. There were primroses in the hedgerows and daffodils in the roadside verges. The best daffodil display was shortly before we reached the course, in front of Fairlawne, Plaxtol, Peter Cazalet's training establishment from where he sent out 'the horse who didn't win the

Grand National', the Queen Mother's Devon Loch who so dramatically and mysteriously sprawled on the run-in with the 1956 race at his mercy.

The last fence on the point-to-point course was beside the open ditch that was taken on the previous two circuits. One day I was standing beside it, rigged out in the said jodhs, when an old man (well, he looked old) said to me, 'You riding in the ladies race, then?'

'No, but I will one day.'

No doubt he smiled to himself, but in later years I was to score there three times; it was also the scene of my worst point-to-point fall.

I longed to be allowed to ride. Wait until you are seven, my parents said. Every Christmas Eve we lined up to make a wish when stirring the Christmas pudding, in reverse age order, Patsy first, then me when I made my annual fervent wish for a pony, then my big brother Tim, followed by Nanny, Margaret and finally Rex, who would make an act of it, burbling mumbo jumbo, gobbledegook that would make us laugh. Then it was out with the ancient sleigh bells (Granny Helen could remember them being on her father, Emery's carriage horse in New York), the reading of '*T'was the Night Before Christmas*' (from an original copy), and finally the hanging of the stockings.

Early Christmases were at Granny Helen's (my mother's mother) at Nevill Park, Tunbridge Wells, where I had cut my knee as a toddler, and it was here that I probably heard my first Mayflower stories.

It was my maternal ancestors John Howland and Elizabeth Tilley who had both emigrated on the famous Mayflower voyage of 1620 – but John 'a lusty young man', was lucky to make it. What he was doing out on deck in one of the many severe storms must remain conjecture but as one of the younger and fitter pilgrims he was probably helping the crew in bringing down some sails to try and run before the gale, and bring some stability to the vessel. Suddenly yet another huge wave, even bigger than the others, tore over the decks; John Howland was swept away like a helpless puppet. Somehow, he managed to grab hold of the topsail halyard and clung to it grimly as down into the depths he dropped many fathoms, falling, falling, eyes tightly shut, mouth closed and cheeks puffed out as he strove to keep some oxygen. Above, other men frantically pulled on the rope; at last, they felt it tighten and with all their strength they hauled John Howland back towards the surface of the tempestuous sea. A boat hook was thrown out to him and inch by wobbly inch, he was winched in.

Before they set foot on the 'promised land' the leading men, John Carver,

William Brewster, Myles Standish, Edward Winslow and William Bradford among them, decided it would be prudent to draw up a charter, the 'Mayflower Compact', often considered the forerunner of the American Constitution. This was a covenant in which the men combined themselves into a civil body politick 'for our better ordering and preservation … to enact, constitute and frame such just and equal laws … from time to time as shall be thought most meet and convenient for the general good of the colony; unto which we promise all due submission and obedience.' It was signed by all free adult males and some though not all servants. John Howland, employed by the man who became the founding fathers' first Governor of their colony, John Carver, chose the pilgrim lifestyle freely; he was one of the first to sign the compact.

Howland was considered one of the most resourceful and enterprising men in the colony. He established himself with a reputation as good, solid, and trustworthy; a man capable at both administration and exploration and within a year, when most of the single young men had died during the bitter first winter, he had become Carver's assistant governor.

John married Elizabeth Tilley, and they had ten children and eighty-eight grandchildren – so by now, there are an awful lot of us descendants about.

On November 21, 1621, the first anniversary of their landing, the pilgrims celebrated the first Thanksgiving, which is now held annually on the fourth Thursday of November.

Tim seemed to be away at school most of my childhood; he was born in the War and Patsy and I were post war glut, only 13 months apart. In later childhood Tim would refer to me dismissively as 'the thin one', (Patsy was the pretty one). And as a young adult he laughed whenever I fell off in a race – but one day I discovered he kept a winning race picture of me in his office. It was nice to know he was secretly proud.

But back to my wish for a pony.

Although we lived in Tunbridge Wells, not far from the Pantiles, our house, Oak Cottage was blessed with a two-acre garden. What made it for me, beyond the croquet lawn, fruit and flowers, was 'the rough'. This was my heaven. It contained two or three 300-year-old oak trees (with a swing hanging from the lower branch of the oldest one), a number of fruit trees and in the spring the ground was golden with daffodils. In November we would have our bonfire potatoes (delicious) and fireworks out there (one time the whole box went up in one go); in the spring we would nibble fresh young hawthorn leaves, and occasionally we made a fire, boiled some water and cooked some stinging nettles. A few paths were mown through the long grass making lovely walks or – as far as I was concerned – pretend racetracks. I made jumps everywhere, and with no pony on the horizon it was Bubbly, our pale cream Labrador (registered name Copperhill Champagne) who was learning to jump them with me. Even my bike could be forced over the smaller poles (I'd learnt to ride on my brother's too big bike by sitting on the rear mud guard instead of the saddle.) I would pedal furiously to make the bike 'jump' over the pole or across a small ditch; I might be pitched forward as I landed, young bones rattling, but then it was on again towards the next, all the time keeping up a running commentary until finally, elated, I crossed the 'finishing' line ('first', invariably), and flung myself into a heap in the long grass, bicycle wheel still spinning beside me. I never did outgrow the pony-mad/tom-boy phase – or the competitive racing spirit.

We were, in spite of this rural oasis, actually very close to the town, and the historic Church of King Charles the Martyr. Built in 1678, it was the first permanent building in the town and when extended in 1690 a stunning plaster interior ceiling was added by Henry Doogood; in the 19th century Queen Victoria was a regular attendee.

Occasionally I joined my mother in walking to church. Except, of course, I skipped most of the way, and I just had to jump all the manhole covers placed at intervals along the red brick pavement. In the paling fence alongside grew what I now know to be bindweed, that perennial foe for gardeners, but then, as far as I was concerned, it was a plant with white flowers that made great trumpets on the end of the nose.

It was a short walk from our house down to there and the famous Pantiles – the colonnaded promenade complete with the Chalybeate spring of iron water (tasted disgusting) and the Common beyond. It was in 1606 that a young nobleman riding through the woods south of Tunbridge discovered a spring, the water of which was rusty in colour indicating its iron properties. Soon fashionable and would-be fashionable people began flocking to the 'wells of Tunbridge', led by the dandy Richard Beau Nash who along with Beau Brummell did much to influence polite society and etiquette of the time; and thus, a legendary and beautiful spa town grew, with many fine buildings designed by Decimus Burton. The coffee houses, lodgings, shops, taverns and gaming houses that sprang up from the spring are today boutiques, antique shops, pubs, restaurants and open-air cafes so it is not that much altered from the original. With the coming of the railways, and the muddles caused by the similarity in names, the ancient town of Tunbridge, straddling the River Medway and guarded by a 13th-century castle, had its spelling changed to Tonbridge to avoid confusion. Meanwhile, in 1909, King Edward V11 added the prefix Royal to Tunbridge Wells, then one of only two English towns with this honour (the other being Royal Leamington Spa, close to Warwick) – and in 2011 this honour was also conferred on Wootton Bassett, Wiltshire. This was in recognition of its residents who all too frequently voluntarily lined its streets as a mark of respect to the corteges of servicemen and women killed in Iraq or Afghanistan. The hearses were being driven from nearby RAF Lyneham to the John Radstock Hospital, Oxford, where their families awaited.

In Tunbridge Wells, just up from the old Pump Room and the Pantiles, was the part where once a year the Fun Fair came to town, and also the Circus. Another annual occasion was the Boxing Day meet of the Eridge Hunt when thousands of townspeople flocked to the Common to see the resplendent sight, the fine horses, the friendly hounds who would happily jump up and lick children, the red and black coats and, in those days, many top hats. Tim was taken when he was little and was asked if he liked it.

'Y-es', he hesitated, puzzled, 'but where's the fox?'

En-famille, including Bubbly, from a snowy meet at the Crest and Gun, Eridge – four duffle coats

The Common was great for rambling and especially for climbing on the outcrop of grey rocks near the top of the Common. The Wellington Rocks were surrounded by sand and had deep crevices to daringly jump across, and steep sides to conquer by climbing to the top; they were great for hide and seek and generally mucking around. Once, when on my own, I walked past a man exposing himself on a bench; I didn't know what it was but instinct told me it wasn't right. I didn't tell anyone, though. The Common was bounded on the top by Mount Ephraim with various hotels which were, I think, mainly lived in by the elderly; the Common was dissected by Major York's Road and a couple of smaller roads. Down near the main road was Brighton Lake and off it to the side away from the town was Nevill Park where Granny lived. There were two cricket grounds, Higher and Lower, and once there had been a racecourse.

A short bike ride away from the house, up a non-vehicular road was the Tunbridge Wells Tennis Club and, above it, the Cricket Ground, so both sports were part of my childhood and I would contentedly watch either for several hours. Tennis week was a recognised Wimbledon warm up and one player we housed was a South African called Thea Hale; my parents and she remained in lifelong contact. Cricket fortnight was another must, Kent v another county and then the big one, Kent v Sussex.

Rainy days: those not much fun indoor days when my nose was likely to be pressed against the window pane and my eyes trying to decipher the garden that I was itching to play in beyond the raindrops.

'If you go out, you'll catch your death of cold,' we'd be told, but I was lucky and never got colds as a child. Now, in middle age – all right, I refuse to use the word old, I'm just older than I used to be – if I get a drenching a chill often follows. Poor Patsy used to get tonsillitis and eventually, as a teenager, had her tonsils out. Sometimes on those 'indoor' days we would get out Mum's wind-up gramophone and listen to her 78 LPs, *Red Sails In The Sunset, Smoke Gets In Your Eyes* and another perennial favourite, *Harbour Lights*. On a Saturday morning we would listen to Children's Favourites presented by 'Uncle Mac' on the Light Programme. I'd often heard Dad admire Bing Crosby so one day I sent off a request for Bing to sing *The Ugly Duckling*; this was Danny Kaye's record, but at that time I just assumed that any singer could sing any song.

Before I was seven there were three world events that I was well aware of: Edmund Hillary's scaling of Mount Everest; the Coronation of Queen

Elizabeth 11 - Tim was allowed to go to London with our parents to see it while Patsy and I stayed at home with Nanny to view it on the (somewhat snowy) new-fangled television (black and white); and the first sub four-minute mile of athlete Roger Bannister.

The morning of my seventh birthday dawned at last. Presents were always kept a secret from us, and all the better for it; those today who ask for something and know they'll get it miss out on the element of surprise, on the other hand, they don't get stuffed away unwanted. Likewise, I remember a Christmas when we were young and times were tight and our parents said, apologetically, that they weren't able to get us much that year. Yet all I remember is opening masses of parcels; I know now that they contained gifts, games, etc, that were not very expensive but a small child is too young to understand value versus quantity and to me it was magical.

On that seventh birthday – my special one, having been born on the seventh of the month – the parcel in front of me gave off a slight but intriguing smell. Excitedly I tore open the paper and there, in front of me, was my first pair of jodhpurs (wide-thighed, of course) and a brown velvet cap. I was so overcome with joy that I was dumbstruck; I literally didn't know what to say and was, temporarily, completely unable to remember the words 'thank you'. All I could come out with was 'yes' and repeated it several times. Apparently, my parents had nearly given me only the jodhs but had been persuaded by the sales assistant to include the cap, something for which they were to be eternally grateful.

The Brown Felt Hat – and All That

Those first weekly riding lessons, on Sundays during school holidays, were on a little iron grey pony called Muffin at the stables of Miss Betty Insole (surprising how long-un-thought-of names come back).

I had my first fall off Muffin, a tumble really. Something made him stop dead as we were walking along the road and I simply fell off, no harm done. People were quick to come out with 'it takes seven falls to make a rider'.

When I was eight, we moved to the Peates' Moat Farm Stables on the edge of Tunbridge Wells beside Hargate Forest, part of the Eridge Estate. It was the beginning of a lifelong friendship and was to have a great influence on both my parents' and my lives. Angela Peate would take us out for a ride on a Sunday morning, usually about six or eight of us. One of the pupils who came there as a white-faced 15-year-old was Hugh Robards and he went on to become a renowned huntsman, notably of the Limerick Hunt.

Moat Farm (there was an old moat around a mound in an orchard) was a lovely old traditional stable yard, mellow red bricks for about four feet round the perimeter, a sturdy mounting block in the stoned centre, and a clock tower in the centre of the middle row of stables. A short chestnut-lined avenue led into it with two little orchards on either side, and a further three fields that were lined by houses marking the boundary of Tunbridge Wells (inevitably those fields have also been covered in housing for many years now); on the opposite side of the road, it was East Sussex. There was a white-painted flintstone house in keeping with the yard, lived in by old Mrs Peate, permanently thin as a rake, and Angela, big smile, distinctive voice. Mrs Peate did the accounts and every receipt went out with a penny stamp on it (or was it 2d?). Guy, the older and more serious of the two sons, was slim with a wide grin and memorable laugh and Jeff, fuller faced, wavy hair, tall, charming, and fun-loving, both rode in point-to-points. They also loved shooting and Guy, a considerable ornithologist, had a passion for the island of Mull off the west coast of Scotland. When 'racing' round our garden I was Guy and Patsy was Jeff. Many years later, I believe, their children would play a similar game pretending to be Anne and Patsy. Jeff married the eternally beautiful Penny Riches, a cover girl for Vogue who would look glamorous even on the coldest, muddiest days. Guy was to become my icon (and my mother's too, truth to tell,) and he was to teach me to race-ride.

The stud groom was called Jack. He always looked old but kind, and one of his jobs was to operate the (now long defunct) chaff-cutting machine. After riding we would help the girl grooms clean the tack and muck out the ponies and, of course, groom them. One 'girl' was a woman called Clare who used to keep her hair in a long plait over her head, halo-fashion; she was quiet but pleasant. The tack room was square and the only part of the four walls not lined with saddles and bridles was the door and a glass cabinet to its side containing a number of red rosettes. A gas stove was lit in the centre so the room was always warm; we cleaned the saddles on a saddle horse and then they were lifted up on to the wall racks for us; the bridles to be cleaned hung from a three-pronged hook from the ceiling. The smell of leather and polish remains with me as pleasurable, but not the gas. I don't think I ever saw Jack in the tack room but it seemed to be a meeting place for everyone else. Next to the tack room was a row of three stalls, with a stable (loose box) at the far end. The ponies would be brought in from the field to the stalls, tethered for grooming and tacking up, and then turned out again afterwards, so they were never permanently tied up. Brick walls and wrought iron railings divided the stalls, as was the way in 19th and early 20th century hunting stables.

For us there was never the dreariness of riding round a school or arena. Instead, we were taken for hacks through the forest, taught to rise to the trot, not to let the ponies eat the bracken – which grew above them in high summer – and to grip with our knees. Occasionally we had to put a leaf between each knee and the saddle and pretend it was a five-pound note, a large sum of money then; today I believe it is no longer the fashion to grip with the knees but it never did me any harm! We may not always have been very 'correct' in our riding (and I struggled to 'use my legs' as I was bidden) but at least we had Fun. We were never barked at to do this, that or the other – and we never got bored or put off riding. It was not until well into adult life that I discovered what 'changing the diagonal' means – and it's not turning diagonally across the arena to start going in the opposite direction.

It was in Eridge Park that we used to have our Pony Club rallies, but before that I'd had my second fall.

This one was far more serious. We were riding along Bunny Lane two abreast and for the first time in my eight-year-old life I was on the outside at the back – and feeling a little proud that I was deemed good enough to be there; I was riding Edwina, a nice chestnut mare. Others amongst the group were Edward, a smart bay New Forest pony with black points, like Edwina about 12 hands high, as were the brown Tiddler and Honey, a rotund dun. One of the bigger ponies was Lance, who had a hogged mane. Others come into the story later on.

Anyway, we were trotting along when suddenly a deer bounded from out of the woods and onto the road, frightening Edwina. She spun round and bolted down the road. Not surprisingly I fell off, but this time at some speed, and again on the road. I skidded along the sharp chippings, spraining my ankle, ripping a square patch of velvet off my riding cap, and severing a piece of my hair plait. There is no doubt that the cap saved my head from injury.

I believe I was taken back in a car though being decades before mobile phones, I don't know how it was summoned; I may have simply walked back on the pony.

My first day's hunting came when I was ten, in the vast forest of Bayham Abbey, the second big estate around us after Eridge. The joint-Master and huntsman was Major R.E. 'Bob' Field-Marsham, one of the great characters of the hunting world. Tall and willowy, a bad back curtailed his riding career but he remained an enthusiastic hound breeder.

"When I come back to life, I want it to be as a stallion hound, the best life on earth," he used to say in a voice as resonant as the hounds' music. The Eridge Hunt contained much woodland, with only small grass fields in between, making long runs virtually impossible; so, it was ideal for beginners or those slowing down a bit. The fields contained heavy clay soil that made the mud extremely difficult to brush off both jackets and ponies, and the woods held some 'bottomless' areas as well as many overhanging branches that frequently sported ladies' hairnets; they also caused a good many painful twangs across faces. But, oh, the sound of the hounds' music deep in Bayham woods; stirring, spine-tingling. Magical. No wonder I have loved it ever since.

I continued to love the hacking at home, too. Of course, you do get the purists who from a young age will always want to do things just so, but for me the magic was in the forest rides. In places there were wide fire-breaks where we could have a canter but I enjoyed best the ruggedness of the meandering paths, the silver birch branches tracing their way over mossy glades, the bracken, the occasional fallen log, the pine trees. At the far end of the forest, we came out onto Bunny Lane, through one of the Eridge Estate's huge (it seemed) heavy white gates, bearing the A for Abergavenny above the hinge end. From there we would hack along the lane for a bit and then turn back into Hargate via another big gate and up what was originally a carriage drive, lined on both sides by dense rhododendrons.

When we were older, we could cross over Bunny Lane into the Estate proper, close by the Eridge Foxhounds, kennelled so deep into the woods that neither noise nor smell could ever offend anyone; it was a clearing in the middle of the woods, with the huntsman's house (not dissimilar to the Peates'), and the tiny, quaint 16th century whipper-in's cottage, very beautiful but doubtless minute to live in, very dark and completely devoid of mod-cons. I saw it again 40 years later when the trees surrounding it were down and the tiny cottage was now a substantial country house; the kennels had ceased existence in the early 1980s when the hunt amalgamated with the Southdown. Behind the hunt complex was another old carriage drive that had a tiny lodge at its entrance off Bunny Lane and another where the thick rhododendrons and old trees opened out into the deer park and, a bit further on, the Castle; the massive structure was demolished and rebuilt as a manageable modern home in 1937, but remained known locally as 'the castle'.

The Marquess and Marchioness Abergavenny lived in the Castle; Lord 'Ab' (John) was an approachable and highly able hunt chairman, 'counsellor' to any villager who called to see him and seek wise advice – and the Queen's personal representative at Royal Ascot. I glimpsed enough to see something of the responsibilities he took on by virtue of his birth and with this sort of person in the House of Lords, giving of their time and wisdom, Britain could always remain a great country. Lady 'A' (Patricia) was joint-Master of the hunt and was equally approachable. I think she was a Lady-in-Waiting to the Queen. She awarded me the hunt button when I was 17. They had four children, two older girls who we therefore didn't know well (Lady Vivienne married crack Irish amateur rider Alan Lillingston who won the 1963 Champion Hurdle on Winning Fair, and Lady Anne who married event rider Martin Whiteley). But Harry, Earl of Lewes, and Lady Rose were our age and so part of the Pony Club scene and lots of fun we all had together. Rose was always bubbly, and one day after a fall on her butt the instructor said, 'Well, it's well covered'. Rose retorted, 'But it still hurts!'

Nicholas and Emma Soames, grandchildren of Winston Churchill, were also our age and regulars with the Eridge. If my memory is correct, I think Nicholas was fourteen when he broke a leg skiing and during the time off ballooned in weight to look very like his father Christopher, who was married to Mary, daughter of Sir Winston Churchill. They lived at Hamsell Manor, close to Eridge. In time, Nicholas followed his father and grandfather into politics, but not early in his career.

It was a harsh sadness when Harry Lewes died from leukaemia at the age of 17. At the time I was on a secretarial course in London and, sitting on the Tube, suddenly I saw a picture of Harry, dressed as a Queen's page, staring out at me from another passenger's newspaper. In those days, leukaemia was incurable.

That left his cousin, Guy Nevill, as heir to the Eridge Estate; he kept a grey pony called Madame Souri at the Peates but sadly it got colic and died. In 1992 Guy himself died, from an Aids related illness, aged 47. He had been one of a dozen guests at my 21st birthday dinner at Quaglinos, followed by a West End theatre. He rode in a few point-to-points, and had a nice grey horse called Providence; in later years he ran an art gallery in London.

* * *

One of the most memorable weeks of our pony days was the annual Pony Club camp at Plumpton racecourse in Sussex, where our ponies lived in the racecourse stables at the top of the hill and the girls slept in the weighing room. Some of us, aged around 13, swooned over a boy called Simon, one of the lads whose billet for the week was the racecourse changing room.

One of the outings was to the now long defunct Lewes racecourse where Australian jockey Arthur 'Scobie' Breasley rode the first five winners. We also ran in a foot race around Plumpton racecourse. Did I, National Velvet style, ever dream that one day I would race round there for real? Nearly two decades later, I loved being a small part of the early girls riding round NH courses; Fontwell, with its unique figure-of-eight steeplechase course, was my favourite, but Plumpton, nestled beneath the Southdowns, holds special memories from the Pony Club camp onwards. One of those later memories is of the Madhatters Charity Flat Race, the brainchild of Plumpton's chairman Isadore Kerman whose Kybo horses graced the top

National Hunt races in those days. The story goes that his mother used to end her letters to him at prep school with the initials KYBO; apparently this stood for 'keep your bowels open.' It was the first public ride for HRH Prince Charles, the Prince of Wales, and he finished second to racecourse commentator Derek 'Tommo' Thompson. A character trainer called Jim Old kindly lent me a horse to ride called Linatea and, at 50-1, he ran the race of his life to finish fifth.

The Madhatters Charity flat race at Plumpton. l-r: HRH Prince Charles, 2nd; the author; Derek Thompson, winner

* * *

It was when I was ten that at last a horse came into our family. No, not a pony for me, but a point-to-pointer for Margaret. Amazing that it had taken her that long, really, given her love of the sport, and of betting, for that matter. One day I came home from school to see a big note in the kitchen containing one word, CREPELLO. He had just won the 1957 Derby, so I was ten, and Margaret had placed a bet on him. Bless her, Mum never did know much about horses (other than on the racing pages), but she loved nothing more than to see her colours go round and to have a little bet. It was a good while before she attained her first winner, but a more loyal owner there could never have been.

Her first horse rejoiced in the name Buachalan Buidhe (Gaelic for yellow boy) – the pronunciation of which was the bane of Kentish bookmakers, 'butjch-a-lun buddy' being their favoured version.

Buachalan Buidhe, Margaret's first racehorse – his name was the bane of Kentish bookmakers' lives, pictured with stud groom, Jack. Photo Margaret Holland

Of course, he came from Ireland, as did the second one, a mare called Royal Catch. Margaret's notebook tells me Royal Catch had 'won several races in Ireland', but point-to-pointing's annual, the 'bible' for the sport, states she once finished third in a hurdle race. She eventually arrived at Tunbridge Wells West station having somehow been lost on a siding for four days and her legs never did recover from the too-tight bandages that had been on her all that time. Neither of these two ever won but 'Bookie' or

'Baked Beans' once finished third, earning Margaret the princely sum of £5. But having runners added to the day out watching Mum's orange and green colours whizzing around for at least some of the course. She briefly owned a rogue of a horse called North Atlantic; he followed a distant second (earning her £10) with two run-outs, a refusal and a fall after which she wisely sold him out of racing. So, it was ironic that in due course the new owners ran him again, and he promptly brought down Margaret's Tarkaotter.

* * *

At ten, off I went to boarding school. I was so looking forward to it (Mum and Nanny must have done a brilliant P.R. job on me), even though before I went my plaits were cut off, leaving me with short, straight, very plain hair. I marched up and down the landing corridor of Oak Cottage, a little case in hand, pretending I was there: Battle Abbey, Battle, Sussex, site of the Battle of Hastings and William the Conqueror's successful invasion of England in 1066 – and all that. Margaret had been a pupil there and it was simply a part of life that I would go there, too. I tried on the uniform, thick brown tweed skirt and jacket, thick brown knickers, thick long fawn socks, cream coloured warm Viyella shirt and brown and cream striped tie – oh, and brown felt hat, and stout lace-up leather shoes. We even had to wear this at the start of the summer term until at length it was deemed warm enough to wear summer uniform, quite a pretty gingham dress, short socks and sandals and a blazer and Panama hat. Mind you, the dormitories were freezing cold.

At St Leonards'-on-Sea, Tim with his sisters, Anne and Patsy.

21

Point-to-point picnic, and the car bar for the adults

*Plaits gone and boarding school started, here with Nan, Tim,
and Patsy (left.)*

But oh, the shock when I got to school. I had my eleventh birthday during my first term. Having so looked forward to it, I hated it. Just didn't seem to fit in. Strangely, for a school full of daughters of the well-heeled, I was the only pony-mad one in my year and that didn't help, but neither did I do my cause any good by loving work (still do), or by telling the others, innocently, that I was anaemic. Also, for some reason, I'd gone a term later than the rest, and they had all already settled in, and formed their friendships, and so on. Later, I was to develop wicked acne, which lasted well into adult life.

For whatever reason, I was always the target of unmerciful teasing and yet – and yet, one time after about a couple of years there, Matron came along and said she thought I looked as if I had a headache and perhaps, I should go to bed. My head felt fine, but of course did as I was bid. A few days later, (I think perhaps it was my birthday), the whole form gave me a present. They had got Matron to pack me off and then clubbed together and raised enough to buy me a fashionable full, stiff, lace petticoat. Very touching. The usual practice was to give little individual gifts to friends on birthdays. I still have a number of them, mostly china miniature animals: little rabbits, dogs and bears, white with a splash of colour on an ear, a paw, a tail; they cost sixpence. Little white horses cost 1/6d and the bigger ones, for special friends, cost 2/6d.

The town of Battle was always full of visitors in the summer, and there were many tourist shops. Also, a black and white timbered teashop, the Pilgrim's Rest that made the best fudge that I've ever tasted anywhere; more than fifty years on and I can still salivate remembering it. Not that we got out very often; I think it was every other Tuesday afternoon, in pairs, and when we were seniors on a Saturday afternoon as well (if not playing in a match), still in pairs.

The school grounds were enclosed by a huge wall, about fifteen feet high, and the entrance was an arched gateway with massive heavy gates, on each side of which was a tall turreted tower. At the top of one of these was our art classroom, with lofty views across the town one way and over the school building and tennis courts the other. I think the gatekeeper lived in the other tower; he wore a uniform and cap and had a built-up boot on one foot. There was a building next to the art tower that was our primitive gym. I can remember envying the local secondary modern school's state-of-the-art facilities, including a swimming pool. Our facilities, such as they were (and certainly no pool), were character building!

Some of the classrooms overlooked the abbey ruins that were open to the public. Sometimes I would gaze out of the window at the groups of visitors being escorted by a guide. Then he would stop and point to the school building.

"Now you see those nine arches along there," he would intone in a lovely burr, pointing up to the part where I was sitting, and then on he would go with the history.

We were allowed out on Sundays, from after church that ended about 12noon, until 6pm, even in the light summer evenings. If anyone returned so much as five minutes behind time they'd be in trouble, although as the headmistress, Miss Gifford, had been my mother's form mistress in her day, Margaret always reckoned it was she who got the rocket if we were late.

The parents drove down almost every Sunday and took us out to a nearby country hotel for a traditional Sunday lunch followed by a walk in the woods with Bubbly; we picked primroses in season, and Nanny usually came too. I wonder if she had days off and I don't recall her ever having a holiday, except those with us but even then, she was 'on duty'; she probably had Sundays off, certainly it was Margaret who cooked the Sunday lunch, roast and all the trimmings, followed by perhaps an apple pie and custard, or steam pudding or, one of Dad's favourites, treacle tart. Margaret would tease him that he even put sugar on that, but I don't think he did really.

There wasn't time to go home on those Sunday afternoons and Margaret always said it would be unsettling, and that weekly boarding would be even more so; I didn't agree then (but naturally didn't say so, whatever our parents said went), and I don't agree now, half a century later. School would have been far more tolerable with week-ends at home.

* * *

This was a feeling that only increased with the passing years, especially once I at last had a pony of my own. Having wished for one for so long, with never so much as a hint that the parents would relent, my thirteenth Christmas had given me no clue of what was to come. I was now riding a slightly bigger riding school pony in the school holidays, a grey called Quicksilver, on whom I'd won a prize at a gymkhana in Eridge Park and had formed quite an attachment to . She was the perfect pony, with no quirks, able to jump a reasonable course, clever at gymkhana games, and reliable out hunting.

As a young teen, I had finally given up my annual Christmas wish when stirring the pudding, opting instead, I think, for my first pair of stockings (they had seams in those days and were held up by suspender belts), when my prayer finally came true. There, before me at the stables, was a liver chestnut called Shindy, standing about 13.1hh with a hogged mane and a roman nose; and for Patsy there was Quicksilver.

Shindy hadn't been at the stables long so little was yet known about him. We soon discovered he was a right devil, with a healthy buck in him! In addition, he used to put his tongue over the bit and bolt. Not quite the ideal first pony, but of course I adored him. I would go along singing, 'Shindy, oh Shindy, Shindy won't let me down' (to the tune of Cindy); even as I sang the words my heart knew he would, but nevertheless I bought a sparkling brass name-plate for his headcollar with my pocket money (and eventually gave it away to his new owner).

Shindy, my first pony, used to buck and bolt – but he stood OK for the heavy Abergavenny gates.

He bucked me off many times; my worst fall from him came one Christmas Eve when I was bucked off riding bareback, flat on my back and damaged my sacroiliac joint; it has caused spells of bother on and off down the years, more on nowadays.

There was one time when we were at a little show where I'd entered a jumping competition. We jumped the first fence fine but as we landed Shindy saw the exit ahead of him; that was it, out he bolted. I rode straight back in but of course we were eliminated and not allowed to continue.

After it was discovered that he was putting his tongue over his bit a vulcanite 'tongue' was added to his Pelham bit to try and curb the habit. Don't think it made much difference to his behaviour though.

Nevertheless, Shindy taught me not only a lot about how to sit on a horse but also on how to accept disappointments.

Eventually he was traded in for a black mare of about 14hands who I named Kerrynane (after Derrynane beach in Co Kerry). She was a slug and had to be kicked continuously to make her go at all. The parents were advised to get her because it was thought I'd lost my nerve but having experienced that in later years I know I hadn't.

Kerrynane, by contrast did not do much at all.

Still, she stayed with us a year. Then one day I had a ride on Mr. Linnet at the Peates'. We were in the little orchard behind the stables with not much room to do anything but when I kicked him to canter, he let out a 'whoopee!' and I was hooked.

He had spark! Soon Kerry was sold and Linnet was mine. Lucky me. A Welsh cob of 14.3hh, a shining dark brown, with black points and white socks, he remained in our family for the rest of his life and he is the one who really got me going. Riding, hunting, competing all came alike to him and he was such fun to ride; he would jump anything, and he really wouldn't let me down. Eventually he was passed on to Patsy and then finally to Tim who was by that time grown up and farming in Wales where he and Linnet hunted for many years (Tim being a later starter to riding), and where he lived out his last years in retirement on the slopes above Pendine.

It was Mr Linnet who got me going, and he stayed in the family for the rest of his life. Three short years later I rode in my first point-to-point, at Brooklands on a cold Romney Marsh, kitted in hunting breeches and boots.

Mr Linnet was followed by a cob, Sir Toby, and he also stayed with us for many years, and once we had the point-to-pointers he could be used as a lead horse when schooling, or for teaching me to get my lower legs forward over a drop fence. Next came my first small thoroughbred Figleaf, by which time I was seventeen and about to leave school.

It was probably also the last year of many family holidays in County

Kerry, too, where Patsy and I always enjoyed 'eyeing up the talent' amongst the other families there who had teenage children/boys, to enjoy communal evening family games, to chat about the fish caught that day, or to swim from Derrynane beach and generally muck around with.

Leaving school was the most significant moment of my life so far; the last year had been by far my best when at last I 'had all the privileges and broke all the rules' – I recall Sobrani cigarettes being sent to me by a boy, I think they had black paper with a gold band and were considered very sophisticated. (Luckily, that was about my sum experience of smoking.) I had enjoyed being part of the 1st X11 in lax (lacrosse) and had done well in exams, after which we were taken for a day out to Wimbledon; there was rather a dishy German playing called, I think, Wilhelm Bungert, and he wore a pastel blue V-neck jumper. For all of us girls leaving Battle Abbey there was a huge feeling of emotion that after seven years we were finally to be released into the big wide world. We scrabbled around writing 'memoirs' in each other's books and promises to keep in touch, and a fair number still do. Almost every entry in mine was from class mates apologising for the way they had teased me.

Firstly, I spent three months in Salzburg to learn the language, German lessons at school having been a non-event, followed by a year's secretarial course in St Godric's College, Hampstead, (father still being adamant that horses were not to be a way of life).

But I was now able to take the point-to-pointers out hunting. One day, there was a good-looking man on another point-to-pointer, so it was easy to begin chatting about my favourite sport, and my dreams of taking part.

IV

Sent Away

Neither horses nor farming had been in either family's recent ancestry.

Mine was one more of the sea, with several generations of naval service on my father's side, and of the historic sea crossing on the Mayflower to America in 1620 on my mother's.

For some reason T, born in London, had from an early age wanted to do nothing else other than farm and, like me, he stuck to his ambition.

He left war-time school (evacuated to Chipping Camden, Gloucestershire,) with the School Cert, in which at least six exams, including English and maths, had to be passed, pre-dating O levels, and then GCSEs; it was known as matriculation. He went straight from that into working on a farm near a then small village called Milton Keynes, created a city in 2022. The actual even smaller village that he worked in has long since been subsumed by that huge new-town conurbation, where the powers that be decided to install concrete cows for people to view when arriving by train.

For T it was the real thing. He bore to the grave a crooked nose caused by a kick from a cow. Milking, then as now, meant early mornings, long hours and every now and then a certain amount of danger. Cows kick to the side and can be very quick and accurate. The same can be said of a thoroughbred horse but generally they kick straight out behind, with a long reach. But they can occasionally 'cow-kick' out to the side. I was kicked on the arm once when I was leading a horse, holding the head-collar rope beside his shoulder, yet he managed to reach me. This wasn't out of viciousness but because it was the first time out of his stable in three months, having been injured and confined to box-rest. With a horse it is usually high jinx and a feeling of well-being, and only rarely through a nasty temperament.

It was the end of the War when T started this first job and food was still very much rationed. But for a tall, lean teenager working long and physical hours he would wolf down a whole loaf of bread at every tea-time. There were also work horses on the farm and these are probably what gave him his first love of these great and noble creatures.

We continued to meet out hunting, and on a bright spring afternoon in beautiful Eridge Park he kissed me for the first time– not the easiest thing to achieve leaning across from one fidgety horse to the birthday girl on another… I was nineteen.

It was a considerable number of months later that I realised he was married; he never actually told me so, but it became apparent. When he mentioned he had a son of eleven, Tim, and a daughter, Lesley, of 13 it took a few moments to sink in. Lesley was just six years younger than me. Today, in my 70s, she still sends me a Mothering Sunday card, and Tim, for many decades a resident of South Africa, also keeps in touch.

Divorce was a much slower process in those days. At 20, I was sent away by my parents to my godfather in Australia for me 'to make sure of my feelings for T.' Coming-of-age was 21, and I had no say in the matter.

Before then I had ridden in a few point-to-points. My longed-for first ride came just a couple of weeks after that secret first kiss on my nineteenth birthday. It was 1966 and Arkle had won his third majestic Cheltenham Gold Cup two days earlier. There was one adjacent hunts ladies race on the card; most hunts were adjacent to about six others so that was it: six or seven rides only in a year for female riders. The season ran from February 1 to the end of May, and runners had to have qualified by hunting 'fairly and regularly', for a minimum of eight times. The ladies race was always the highlight of the day and the male spectators loved it. Pretty, curvaceous blondes competing alongside weather-beaten women, but what they really liked was the speed of it. Of course, men claimed it was because the girls couldn't hold their mounts but the truth was that the ladies race was run at 11 stone, and all men's races at 12stone7pounds and so, with less weight to carry, the ladies race was usually the quickest.

My mount was Tarkaotter, who a couple of years earlier had fallen at the first in his first race, and promptly won his maiden next time out showing promise for Guy Peate, but he was inclined to be thin and to cough. His early potential, including a second win, degenerated and sometimes he simply ran badly. It was before allergy to dust had really become understood, although eventually he was put on to a peat bedding with miraculous results. Quite how Rex relented into letting me race is unclear but it was probably a mixture of Guy suggesting that Tarka might cope better with the lighter weight and of Margaret's influence, for while always less vocal than my dad, she was nevertheless the one who usually held sway. And she was as proud as punch to have a daughter riding in her bright orange and green colours. It was a mixed emotion for Guy, for while he undoubtedly wanted me to do well, he was at the same time losing his ride.

About a week before my first race, I got a sore throat. It didn't develop into anything, and over the years since I have discovered that if I am nervous about something coming up there it is again: a sore throat. So, I've learnt to dismiss it and get on with things.

We set off for Romney Marsh with all the usual picnic paraphernalia, and this time my kit bag, too. Most of the day passed in a haze and I remember very little of it: only the biting, searing east wind that made it difficult to breathe and nearly impossible in the race (I was probably subconsciously holding my breath anyway); the dark, thick hunting breeches I was wearing instead of white jockeys' breeks; and of 'pulling up' when tailed off last out in the country on the second circuit. Truth to tell the horse pulled himself up; I was a total passenger, and of the first three fences I remember nothing at all.

I do remember T and his friend Les Bowman, the farmer and permit holder for whom T used to ride out, greeting me out in the countryside where I had pulled up, and then melting into the crowd again. It was on Les Bowman's horses that T had first met and subsequently kissed me in those hunting days.

Bowman's racing colours were, I think, black with white spots and a red cap with a white band. They were generally fairly moderate horses – although Orbiquet, once owned by the Queen Mother, was quite a smart ladies point-to-pointer, but I admired him for entering a horse one year in the King George V1 and Queen Elizabeth Gold Cup, the second-most prestigious steeplechase after the Cheltenham Gold Cup, at Kempton on Boxing Day. The mighty Arkle had scared away the opposition and only three were declared, so all Les Bowman's horse had to do was jump round to gain very decent place money. Alas, the meeting succumbed to frost and was abandoned.

My second race was in complete contrast to the first. This was on our local track at Heathfield, East Sussex, the shape of an inverted B and very hilly, so that there was quite a big drop fence (where the landing side of the fence is considerably lower than the take-off; Becher's Brook at Aintree is the most famous example), and two or three 'on the turn'. At the furthest point, at the top of the hill near the farm buildings, was the open ditch, then a line of three, the only straight part of the course, which consisted of the drop fence and the last two. The start was with our backs to the drop fence, so the first two fences were jumped three times and the rest twice. One thing I soon learned was that although the fences looked big when walking the course, it was different when showing the first fence to the horse as I was now looking down on it, and the horse calmly gazing over it.

Soon after the winning post the course bent sharply right and then headed towards another fence before seemingly disappearing over the edge. From this part, the track veered sharply right again on the wrong camber (I once had a spare ride stop dead at the next, sending me over his head and the fence as well to land flat on my back the far side). Then it was into a dip and heading left-handed uphill before once more turning right towards the farm.

The course was as pretty as a picture, with views across the wooded countryside to a windmill, and always lots of primroses. It was so compact that all bar the open ditch and drop fence were right in amongst the crowds who would be rushing across from one fence to another to get close up views of the action.

On that second race ride of mine the favourite was a course specialist called Bebe Fare, a black mare ridden by Ann Underwood for the owner, Richard Thorpe, who was Master of the West Kent Hunt. Tarka was a rank outsider, but this race was for real. I kept my eye on the starter, kicked Tarka the moment the flag fell, and was soon leading. Although a rangy sort of horse he took to the bends well and he never made a semblance of a mistake; this was what I'd always dreamed of! It was only between the last two fences that Bebe Fare collared us to win by a couple of lengths. I was elated, and patted Tarka's steaming neck as I rode him into the second's enclosure.

It was the first of many memorable rides there.

Mike Pelly on Peter O'Sullevan's Stay Friendly, a somewhat less talented full brother to Sir Peter's prolific Be Friendly. Tarkaotter on the right, Robert Wilkins behind. Photo Kent and Sussex Courier

Tarkaotter kept trying to get me into the winner's enclosure. Later in that first season we came to the last upsides a very good horse called White Tarquinne at the Southdown meeting when it was held at Ringmer. We were beaten a short-head! But the next season, although second twice and third twice, brought no victory. Significantly, Tarka had a nosebleed after a run at Charing, beaten a distance in a two-runner race. Arnold Crowhurst, the eminent vet with whom we later became good friends, was a spectator and remarked that the horse probably had an allergy. He should not be on straw and his hay should be fed wet (it was before the days of paper bedding, and before haylage.)

The change to peat bedding and wet hay was to prove a revelation. Before then, I had to 'do my time' in Australia.

* * *

Australia was not a happy experience. I didn't particularly like it (although Perth is a lovely sunny city) and I didn't like the country any better when I revisited 40 years later. So it was that on a damp September day in 1967 I embarked on the Greek passenger liner Ellenis in Southampton. I shared a cabin with four others, an older woman we called Nanny; a lady probably in her forties with short, dark, curly hair; and two who were closer to my age.

One, mysteriously, had had her death certificate signed (she never told us the circumstances), and the other had fallen in love with a black boy and, like me, was being sent away to the other side of the world; she simply accepted she would never see her beau again.

We sailed firstly to Gibraltar, where we spent a day sight-seeing, and then to Piraeus, the port for Athens, where we picked up some 600 Greek immigrants. They had their own quarters on the ship. With the Suez Canal closed to shipping (it was 1967, and it had been closed earlier that year because of the Six-Day War, and then remained closed for eight years, the year of our first lambing), we traversed back along the Med. Then it was out into the Atlantic Ocean where we had the closest thing to an adventure: when at sea, we got used to the motion of the ship and the background drone of the engines. One day they weren't there; we were nearly motionless. Word spread that there was a tanker to starboard with a dangerously ill man on board. Soon nearly 2,000 people were peering over that side instead of being evenly distributed around the ship. That made us list alarmingly! But most disobeyed the tannoy request to move back, and watched in awe as a lifeboat was lowered containing doctor, nurse and crew. The sea looked calm, yet the tiny boat frequently dipped out of view in the swell. Eventually the Indian patient was brought aboard, operated on for peritonitis, and nursed until we docked in Cape Town, South Africa, where we had another one-day stop. Finally, and after an awful lot of sea, we hove-to in Freemantle, the port for Perth, Western Australia, and home of my godfather. Six weeks to sail to the other side of the world and see just three countries for one day each. Gibraltar, Athens, and Cape Town remain etched indelibly in my memory in spite of the brevity of the visits.

There were lighter moments. One special week-end was to a couple who lived in the bush about 100 miles north of Perth. I think their name was Armstrong, and we clicked. It was truly rural, I could lean out of the window to pick an orange, and it was from here that I glimpsed my first kangaroo, a big six-foot boomer. The ranch had a number of polo ponies dotted around it, and a few sheep. I'm not sure how the couple eked out a living, but I do remember their holidays always had to be taken separately, so that the other one remained to feed and look after the animals. The house was little more than a shack, but they dined every night off an antique table with solid silver cutlery, and the walls were adorned with original oil paintings.

My other Australian highlight was again in the countryside, an eagerly-anticipated hunting week-end. For my hosts it was one of just three meets away from kennels during the May to September season, but while traditional

British hunting customs die hard – the Australians use the same terms, and the Melton cloth kit most unsuited to the clime – their usual meets were little more than a social mounted picnic. A typical day would see about 30 followers mounted mostly on rather small Australian horses, a lot of chatter, some canters across the scrub – but scarcely the whiff of a fox, and the riders returned contented to their end-of-day stirrup cups.

It was all very different to the country week-end: at one time I wondered if we would get as far as hunting at all, after spending all day Saturday being entertained; Western Australia meets were usually from 7.30am to 10am on Sundays and 3pm till dusk on Wednesdays. A barbecue lunch followed the 100-mile journey into the hills, the last six of which were on a dirt track, and a round of golf strolled away the afternoon, along with an occasional sighting of a kangaroo. After cooling off with a swim the evening party began, with more barbecues, guitar strumming and singing and then, just when it had to be bed-time, a champagne breakfast. Whether this deludes the cheerful Australians into thinking they will have a Shires-type day on the morrow I did not discover, but wondered instead how I would get aboard my tall New Zealand thoroughbred, let alone stay there.

Just a few hours later, clad in borrowed breeches and bowler, I had left the old, stone ranch-house, and once mounted the strength returned to my knees, and I then enjoyed the tingle of excitement at hearing 'hounds, gentlemen, please!' Keenly I listened for just a glimmer of tongue to reward the huntsman encouraging his hounds. There were few actual coverts to draw for the Western Australian bush extends for miles, uninterrupted save for a few boundary fences.

Hounds pushed through scrub, over fallen branches and across patches blackened by summer fires. The field (the term for the mounted followers) seemed undeterred by the apparent lack of foxes, standing or trotting in small groups chatting under the blue sky, occasionally a pair holding back for a bracing canter to the main party.

Just as the first hound spoke, I glimpsed a large grey animal moving between some gnarled eucalypts, now camouflaged, now spotted again as it bounded swiftly ahead – and the unmistakeable knowledge that the pack was in full cry after a kangaroo. There was no time to tell the Master – a roo can out-run a fox (and most foxhounds) any time – and we were off. Ducking beneath a gum tree, my host flashed past grinning, 'grey fox!'

Soon off the track, we twisted and turned across open bush, my tall New Zealander threading his way, turning like a polo pony in and out of the vegetation. There were no jumps as such, but a horse as sure-footed as any

Exmoor with the speed of a thoroughbred was needed to negotiate the fallen logs, the ditches and twists and turns, and still keep up.

It was a thrilling, exhilarating hour. The 'grey fox' was safe and we had enjoyed a memorable ride.

* * *

Towards the end of my stay my Godfather, a wonderful man called John Rawlinson (he and my father had 'won the war' together), took me right across southern Australia, 48 hours on a train across the Nullabor Plain. It was interesting to watch the vegetation gradually reduce from lush to scant to nothing at all. Then it was to a vineyard north of Adelaide; a flight to Melbourne where we stayed in the Southern Cross Hotel and visited the Melbourne Cup (won that year, 1967, by Red Handed, trained by Bart Cummings for his third of what was to be a record twelve wins in the race;) then on up to Canberra followed by a drive through the Snowy Mountains to Sydney; staying everywhere at the best hotels with fine wine and meals each evening (all of it paid for out of my trust fund, I was to discover a good many years later), and then the memorable flights home via Tahiti and two weeks in America.

Enroute to Tahiti, which is about half way across the Pacific Ocean, the plane encountered a huge storm; gradually the chatter in the cabin became less and less until the only sound was that of sliding objects, slipping glasses and falling books. My neighbour whispered to me he was a member of the Goldfish Bowl Club, exclusive to survivors of aircraft ditching in the sea. I don't know if there really is such a club, but he did his best to reassure me.

The landing strip for Tahiti was on a coral reef, so only water was visible either side of the plane. On leaving the aircraft the sheer warmth and humidity hit me. We were met by beautiful Tahitian girls selling garlands of flowers and shell necklaces; I still have two necklaces.

My first day was with a family, contacts from people I'd met in Australia, and included a magical introduction to snorkelling, and an outdoor dinner party under the palms beside a gently lapping lagoon; it included my first taste of raw fish. The family had taken in a Tahitian girl who had been spurned by her family for having a baby out of wedlock.

The next day I was in a hotel complex comprised of rush-clad huts. That evening I went with another girl from there to the posh hotel in town where there was a spectacular floorshow. Hips swung, flower garlands swayed, and Tahitian faces smiled, all in perfect unison - four men and ten grass-skirted, bikini-clad girls, with good voices. There was a fire-dancer and all the while musicians beat on varying sizes of native drums – and one electric guitar.

Dancing began, and a Maori boy asked me to dance. He spoke no English, I spoke no Maori, and Tahitian French was like a foreign language compared with the 'O' level version. But dancing is dancing and it was fun and the atmosphere great. He asked, in broken English, if he could take me home.

Yes, I said innocently, and my friend, too, please, indicating the other girl.

But he only had a scooter.

Having said yes, I didn't like to go back on my word so off we went. After we'd gone a little way, it spluttered and ground to a halt.

The main part of Tahiti consists of a volcanic cone, rising more than 7,000 feet into the air, its steep sides and thick jungle impenetrable. There is one circular road of nearly 100 miles that runs around its perimeter. Otherwise, there are just a few tracks off to the sea.

Fearing that I was doing exactly what my mother had always indicated, without actually saying, that I shouldn't, I sat like a limpet on the scooter while the young man fiddled with it. Eventually it half-heartedly sparked into life again and we continued in the direction of my hotel.

But then he turned off into one of the tracks that led to the sea. Suddenly I found myself thinking of Mum rather a lot. Pathetically all I kept repeating was the name of my hotel. He pulled up outside a little hut nestled in the palms a few yards before the beach. So that was it. He was going to force me in there and rape me. Once more I repeated the hotel name. And stuck like glue to the scooter.

He disappeared into the hut and came out a few moments later carrying something in his hand. It was a miniature hand-carved bookcase containing three tiny books of Maori-English, English-Maori, and Maori Proverbs. He indicated it was a gift for me, turned the scooter and returned me to the hotel. I never saw him again – but I still treasure the set of little books.

* * *

T and I wrote to each other every single day while I was abroad, and if I'd been sent away for four years I would still have come back to him. Of course, I dreamed of that elusive first point-to-point win, too. It was T who greeted me at Heathrow on my return. I had flown from Sydney to Tahiti and across America with stops in California, Wisconsin, South Carolina and New York, staying with family friends, much the best part of my trip.

I returned to a country brought to a standstill by foot and mouth disease.

My first task was to start earning a living.

I had attended St Godric's Secretarial College, Golders Green after leaving school. Apart from acquiring shorthand and typing to proficient speeds, I also shared a flat with a red-haired girl, Sar, who became a life-long friend. But I came home every week-end bar one when, stuck in London, I felt claustrophobic, missing the countryside – and the hunting. I looked out of the window down on to the snarl of traffic and wondered what on earth I was doing. I was unlike most girls who love a spell of living and working in London.

After college I took two part-time secretarial posts, one for Mike Pelly on Whitbread's hop farms at Beltring, near Paddock Wood, where my duties included booking in the 'hoppers', the families from London's East End who used to come down for the three weeks of hop-picking in September, living in the little tin huts that were dotted about the grounds towered over by some 40 or more magnificent oast-houses, probably the biggest collection anywhere. Every summer the wonderful shire horses that pulled the Whitbread drays through the streets of London came down to Beltring for their two weeks summer holiday. The sight of those gentle giants cavorting around in the fields of freedom is unforgettable: leaping in the air, prancing, pawing, galloping their great big bodies flat out, rolling, eating the grass, attempting to do all of these things at the same time – the Spanish horses of Vienna they might not have been but they were a sight to behold, and one that invariably found its way on to the front page of the local paper.

My other part time job was with Hadlow College of Agriculture and Horticulture just as it opened its pristine doors to its first students – one of whom I recall for having white blonde hair. I worked with interesting staff there; Mr Swan, the principal, his tall, kind deputy, his secretary and the other secretary besides me. Sadly, I see in 2021 that the college has been in administration, and its farm up for sale.

I had had one article accepted in a monthly horse magazine and I had my secretarial diploma, so on my return from Australia I wrote to Frank Chapman, the group editor of the local paper, the *Kent and Sussex Courier*, Tunbridge Wells, to see if there might be a job. I was thinking along the lines of being a secretary who might gradually get some stories accepted, but the next thing I knew I was indentured for three years as a junior reporter! One of the things that came with the job was a dark green van, with a governor on its accelerator making speeding impossible. Another was learning about Life.

Rookie Reporter

A sheltered upbringing and boarding school had not prepared me for the real world. My new life soon bridged that gap.

When I joined there was a robust middle-aged woman called Betty and though she was meant to show me the ropes it was clear she didn't have time for a mere junior. The short and fat Frank Rushman was the sports reporter and the senior reporter, Frank Sellens was based in Crowborough and had been with the paper for about 100 years (or so it seemed - and which eventually turned out to be not far from the truth.) But the sub-editor appointed to keep an eye on me was Bud Evans (who became a BBC Radio 4 Today editor for many years); I'd only been there a short time when he told me he believed I could go right to the top. Exciting times! I revelled in the work and loved unearthing stories, talking to people from all walks of life (somewhat new to me after Battle Abbey and all that), gently encouraging the shy to talk, building confidence between them and me, then transferring the main points from my shorthand notebook into crisp, cogent news stories (adjectives were virtually ruled out, and there could be no flowery writing).

Our copy was typed on large black clackety-clack typewriters, in triplicate, with carbon paper between the sheets, on small strips of paper, about one third of A4 size. We used various shortenings such as t for the, tt for that and o for of – so we had those abbreviations long before the text messaging of today.

After the subs had inserted their editing/printing instructions, a copy of the story was transferred to the comps (compositors) room, a huge noisy room where all the type was still hot metal, and the typesetters put in each letter individually to make up the words and sentences as they would then come out in the newspaper. Behind that room was the enormous warehouse containing the huge reels of newsprint paper rolls. Fascinating to see them metamorphose into the weekly 'rag'.

There was a little tea-lady called Bella who used to do the rounds daily with the tea on a trolley. Bella's trolley was fine for the big print room but mighty difficult for the narrow, twisting stone stairs that led up to the editorial department, where the editor had his hidey-hole in a sort of turret-like office. A few more stairs led to the journalists' and subs' room divided by a screen. The ground floor was front-of-house, for the sale of papers, photographs (the jam for local newspapers) and advertisements (their bread and butter). The building was just up Grove Hill, above Weekes Department Store (Steve Weekes was one of our teenage friends). The store also fronted the main street, Mount Pleasant, with the old Opera House around the corner and Tunbridge Wells Central station opposite.

There was a senior reporter, Gordon Ducker, a Yorkshire man, who married his beautiful blonde long-standing girlfriend and was on honeymoon when I joined; they had been very 'modern' and lived together before they married. Three short months later they separated and Gordon returned to his native county, where he became a respected newsman for the rest of his life. He died in 2008 and had apparently remarried his first wife a year before. But the upshot of his sudden departure was that the brave editor put me in charge of Gordon's (one-man) Tenterden office – I was still on probation! It was only three months since my first-day task of filing a wedding report, to a set style, from a form submitted by connections; not exactly testing.

Tenterden was (and doubtless still is) a lovely town, a little like Marlborough in that it has a very wide main street and seemed to be full of friendly people and thriving businesses.

I thrived on it, too.

When asked, I've always said being a local paper reporter covers anything from the local jumble sale to a murder and all things in between. Just once I had a murder to cover, but as the culprit was caught and charged before our next edition, making the case sub judice, there was almost nothing I could reveal, beyond name, age, address and charge.

Court work was a large part of local journalism and once a week would find me sitting in the local magistrate's court, a place where I saw much of life. Motoring offences made up most of the day's list – the most minor offences were reported, even parking, and then read avidly by the local populace. Occasionally there was petty crime, too.

Parish councils were usually held once a month, except in August, but as my area covered 12 or more parishes it meant many evenings were spent at work. The good side of that was that I could slip off for a couple of hours in the day to ride! Parish councils were 90% of the time dead boring and put me off being a councillor for life, so many of the councillors seemed to comprise jumped up, self-important little people! Just occasionally a genuinely good story came out of them.

Other aspects of trolling round the villages each week included the visit to the local vicar (a diverse lot); rooting through the posters and adverts in village shops for snippets of news or forthcoming dates; visiting the local police station to go through the day book; the annual flower show; inquests and obituaries; and golden weddings. It all gave me a great insight to village life at grass root level.

At first, I was afraid of doing obituaries – I'd once seen a man fall dead off his horse at a hunt meet and I couldn't get it out of my head at night for a year – but the obits of older people were invariably a privilege to write; the widow (usually) would be only too happy to talk about her late husband and I felt able to do his life justice in print. Once, though, I had to visit a young mother whose husband had been killed in a car crash; seeking to make a bit of chat first, I noticed her young daughter with her arm in plaster.

"How did you do that?" I asked, thinking she'd probably had a fall.

"In the accident."

One of the times I wished for a hole to open up and swallow me.

* * *

Eventually, after five years of waiting, and dreaming and planning, T and I were married in the summer of 1971.

We went to Crowborough Registry Office, a fine country house on the outskirts of the Sussex town that is close to Ashdown Forest, home to Winnie the Pooh. The large, graceful room was furnished with polished antiques and comfortable chairs for those witnessing 'the deed'. Long windows, framed by plush plumb velvet curtains let in plenty of light. Beyond were manicured lawns and rhododendron bushes. It was June 23rd, 1971, a Wednesday. I wore a short white dress with white daisies in relief. T loved mini-skirts, the shorter the better, but I was worried that it might be inappropriate. No-one had been with me when I chose it and my confidence was uncertain – but looking at a picture now, with me nicely made up, flowers in a pretty hairdo and small bouquet, I reckon it looked fine.

Wedding day, June, 1971

It was a family only affair and from there we drove to our delightful church of St Alban's in Frant. The rector, the Rev Downing Berners Wilson, a renowned preacher for whom people would travel many miles to hear (and whose daughter Angela was, I believe, in the first tranche of women to be ordained) gave a simple but lovely service of blessing.

We honeymooned in Corfu which in those days was a relatively unknown and unspoilt island. My parents had come to love it, staying in a sumptuous five-star hotel. We were in a then quiet little place called Sidari. One day we hired a scooter to explore the island which was fun – fun, that is, until the return journey when our spare clothes that T had tied onto the back fell off; apparently, I was supposed to have travelled with my head twisted round the whole way to check them – but otherwise the weather was glorious, the sea warm and blue, I learnt to water-ski, and a culinary treat was eating my first lobster.

"Who needs clothes on honeymoon, anyway?"

On our return the parents put on a splendid party for all our friends and relations and then our family home, The Mast Head, rang to the sound of music and merriment, dancing to a live band, and eating and drinking with gusto.

Then it was my move in to Laundry Cottage, the farm cottage T rented that was, co-incidentally, close to Margaret's first English home at Hildenborough. The cottage was typically Victorian, built of solid red brick, and had at one time housed the launderer for the Hollanden Estate. Behind it was Laundry Bungalow that originally had been the actual laundry, and apart from that we were a mile from anyone else. Laundry Cottage had three bedrooms and a nice sized walled garden; T paid a rent of £3 per week for it.

There were three of us because T's son, Tim, was sent by his mother to live with us, so I began married life aged 24 with a sixteen-year-old stepson. I have always felt I owed a lot to his laid-back character that it worked so well, and he is part of the story.

He was tall and lanky, and a pupil at Sevenoaks School. I didn't think of it as a challenge; if he was part of having T, so be it. My first lesson, though, with two large men in the house, was to cook as if for four. Later, Tim loved cooking occasionally – using copious quantities of brandy and cream – and nowadays he is a chef and vintner in South Africa.

Tim had already been a part of my life for a few years. I taught him to ride and on one memorable occasion he brought home a cup from the local Pony Club hunter trials.

Tim, Sir Toby and trophy, hunter trials at Whiligh, Wadhurst

It was when we were still in Laundry Cottage that T had a dreadful point-to-point fall. We'd bought a lovely horse who we named Kilcullen after the Kildare town we'd bought him from, and he was showing promise. He was third a couple of times and on one occasion he fell at the last open ditch at the Eridge and T broke his collar bone but remounted to finish second, to great acclaim in the local paper.

It was at the same fence that he fell again on his next outing there. This time he brought down another horse who, it transpired, had landed on and broken Kilcullen's ribs. At the time, Kilcullen got up ok and appeared fine, but T did not. He lay unconscious on the ground and was conveyed to Pembury Hospital. Naturally I went with him, and returned again the next day by which time he'd come round, but was still somewhat gaga. But unfortunately, Kilcullen had died in the night. His broken ribs had punctured his lungs and they had filled up with fluid causing him to collapse and die.

Sitting with T, who wasn't talking a lot of sense, made me think of it as a practice for when he was old, when naturally I expected to be caring for him. In his more lucid moments, he got out of me that his horse had died. He wanted to me to go to the kennels to see him, and after he'd asked a number of times, I agreed.

Tim was with me during the hospital visit and as we left and walked across the car park, we saw his mother's sports car with his mother and boyfriend in it. Across she marched and announced that she was taking Tim while T was in hospital; with that the two of them literally bundled the six-foot teenager into the tiny back of the car and drove off. I was numbed. Shell-shocked. As if the accident wasn't bad enough. Slowly I walked to my car, in no state at all to drive; cautiously, I drove very slowly back to the empty cottage.

Next day I went, as promised, to the kennels. The huntsman showed me what little remained of Kilcullen, for he had already been dismembered ready for feeding to the hounds. In one corner was a seemingly endless pile of his innards.

The huntsman took me back into his house and gave me the largest gin and tonic I'd ever had in my life.

Tim's mother mainly stayed out of our lives but did one unforgivable thing to her children, by then grown up, when I was expecting George. In a pique of pure spite, she told them they were adopted. Funnily enough, it was Tim's girlfriend who took it worst. Lesley had suspected it since she was a somewhat trouble teenager, when, at 18, she had run off with and married a railway porter. Within a year she had a daughter and 18 years later that daughter had a daughter, making me an exceedingly young step-great-grandmother! Lesley's second child was a son called Darren who was to prove a real good type, building up his own business and, with his wife Nicky, rearing two smashing sons. As a child, Darren loved nothing more than to come down to the farm and spend time with his granddad and me during the school holidays, and learnt to ride a bit on a pony called Goldie.

T's job was, and had been for many years, with MAFF, the Ministry for Agriculture, Fisheries and Food. All T ever wanted to do was farm for himself, and at last we got our chance. It did not exactly go to plan.

Goldie with George and below, also with step-grandson Darren, left.

* * *

Was it less than a year ago, in 1974, that I had taken a short cut home from yet another unsuitable property viewing? I had turned off the Frant to Wadhurst road into a narrow country lane by the entrance to the 19th century Dewhurst Lodge, which apparently hid a magnificent garden behind its well-maintained seven-foot-high brick wall. Half way along the two-mile lane, before it ran steeply downhill through thick woods, there was a small cottage nestled beyond overgrown garden. The cottage was smothered in creepers, climbing roses embraced the arched windows, pretty mellow brick peeped through the honeysuckle and, at its entrance, stood a For Sale sign. And it came along with 55 acres. My heart leapt.

Newlands Cottage as we found it, nestled beyond overgrown garden.

It was part of a larger farm called Great Shoesmiths, owned by a character called Nancy Hunter-Gray; her considerably younger husband was terminally ill with cancer. It was said that he would drink a bottle of Scotch before breakfast, and who could blame him.

Five years earlier Nancy had lost her baby grandson, Martin de Selincourt from sudden infant death syndrome (SIDS). Distraught that a healthy baby should die so suddenly and inexplicably, she donated £200 to Addenbrooke's Hospital, Cambridge, specifically to hold a two-day symposium on the subject. One upshot of this was the formation of the Lullaby Club whose main campaign has been to publicise the need to put babies to sleep on their backs. As a result, the number of deaths from SIDS has dropped by 80%.

We knew none of this when we met Nancy on June 12, 1974, and two days later our offer to buy Newlands Farm was accepted. On August 15 we signed the contract. A day later I had to cover one of those harrowing inquests which were part of my local paper reporting life: a young person had drunk paraquat, a transparent liquid that can look alarmingly like lemonade. It is deadly poisonous, but it takes three weeks for the victim to die. The only hope is to swallow quantities of Fullers earth, or even just earth from the ground, immediately after ingesting it.

Just over a week later we completed the farm purchase, truly a dream come true. Within days we were obtaining quotes for damp proofing, calling in a pest controller and picking plums from our one prodigious tree, selling some fresh to the local store and making jam out of yet more.

And then it was another awful inquest, this time of three nuns who had driven down the wrong side of the not-long-opened Tonbridge bypass. They were killed instantly.

One impression I took away with me, apart from the obvious tragedy, was of the elderly couple who had been driven into. I had thought how lucky that they hadn't also been killed, but when they were called as witnesses, I was shocked by their states, both mental and physical from the injuries sustained. Their lives had been literally shattered.

It was the era of the three-day week, of two general elections, a state of emergency in Northern Ireland, and extensive Provisional Irish Republican Army bombing of the British mainland, but things like that were not on our minds then.

On that June day, when I first set eyes on it, Newlands Cottage was, as I was to learn, devoid of public services: no gas; water was piped privately from the local Bayham estate, no mains drainage (a septic tank saw to that need) and no mains electricity. This was provided at whim by a temperamental, oily generator in the garage which we had to crank into life when needed.

Inside, the small kitchen housed an ancient Rayburn supplying hot water and cooking facilities if properly stoked up. The two tiny bedrooms had sloping ceilings, creaky floors and arched windows looking out onto the surrounding woods and fields, a haven for wildlife.

Nearby, the wood was a mass of wild flowers, at that time mostly foxgloves whose pendulous pink flowers peered above the thick carpet of still fragrant bluebells. Here and there were clumps of rushes leading to a corner where a sleepy pond revealed bucketsful of frogspawn, overlooked by a mighty beech branch sweeping gracefully down, curving over the pond as if protecting all the wildlife in it. Further on, the profusion of wild flowers gave way to a glade, an enchanting dell where there was sure to be a fairy ring of toadstools. The ground was a soft, spongy brown made by the fallen twigs of another beautiful beech above, its nuts and last autumn's leaves crunching as we walked. Oak saplings sported branches of oak-apples and the sun filtered through the most beautiful of greens, that of a beech in late spring/early summer, etched against the shiny, dark bark of the trunk. A fallen branch was too tempting: I skipped, ran and jumped high over it, just as I used to as a child.

* * *

Even before the For Sale sign came down, we were making plans, deciding sheep would be the best proposition on its sloping acres. Family Planning is easy and extremely predictable with sheep. You simply keep the rams away, sex-starving them until a pre-determined date, while the ewes 'flush' on lush grass. It was one part of the enterprise that needed no help from us.

We bought 200 traditional Romney (Kent) ewes, a large (and therefore quite heavy) dual purpose breed known both for its long wool and meat. We aimed for April lambing, to be after the worst of winter and just as the spring grass and sunshine could be expected. T decided that for the winter months they would be put out to keep, that is, we would pay so many pence per animal to another farmer whose land they would graze; this would give our own land a rest and a chance to grow fresh spring grass, perfect for birthing ewes needing good young grass to ensure they produced enough milk for their lambs. But easier said than done – it proved mighty difficult to find winter keep, and we ended up with lots of little plots scattered around East Sussex and West Kent.

Our five rams, each bearing a coloured 'raddle' on its chest, made swift work of willing females. To make it easy to remember, the tups (rams) were put in with the ewes on November 5, to result in lambs tumbling into the world after their 146-day gestation period from April 1, ironically All Fools Day.

Before all that, there were the summer jobs like hay to make and straw to cart and the cottage to make habitable before we could move in.

Our horses were safely out to grass on their summer holidays by then. My mother, Margaret, also had a small farm at Frant, just a few miles away, which was where the horses 'summered', a well-earned tonic of 'Dr Green' after their winter and spring exploits of hunting and point-to-point racing.

While Margaret's first point-to-pointer had cost £12 a week in livery at the Peates, on the outskirts of Tunbridge Wells, she now nearly always had two, and then the mare Royal Catch was put to stud and so there started being her offspring, plus there was Rex's hunter and, on grass keep, our two ponies, for my sister Patsy and me. It was logical to look for a country house with land. Patsy and I were now well capable of looking after the horses, especially once we had left school. The parents found the ideal place in The Mast Head, Frant, a picturesque village in East Sussex, three miles south of Tunbridge Wells.

Rex Holland on Redskin with the Eridge Hunt. Parkinsons Disease curtailed Rex's career but a good cob kept him going.

Frant village has an exceptionally large village green, some beautiful houses and church, a couple of pubs and a couple of shops. It was on a ridge overlooking yet another part of Eridge Park, in particular Whitehill, one of my top five favourite places on earth. Whitehill was entered from Frant village by a lodge with a big, heavy Abergavenny white gate that opened into a rhododendron-lined old carriage drive. To the left of the gate the land rambled steeply downhill to a stream that connected a couple of lakes as if by a ribbon; the hill was covered in bracken, small trees, occasional mighty beech trees and silver birch, with a few glorious rides winding their way round and down the hill, covering many wild and rugged acres. On the far side of the stream the land had been grubbed and turned into arable, but with a number of mature oak trees remaining. The stubble used to make a wonderful canter when training the point-to-pointers. Beyond that, by now two or so miles from Frant, going parallel with and then past my parents' small farm, was Saxonbury wood, again very pretty with beautiful paths through it. In spring it was a heady blue with the scent and sight of bluebells. It came out the far side onto a tiny little lane and even further on from there was some forestry with wide fire-breaks cut into it that again made excellent canters, especially for ex-racehorses jaded by the routine, the big stables and the expanse of Newmarket or Lambourn. We acquired a number of such horses at Ascot Sales and would bring them home to our small yard, never numbering more than four, take them hunting, and riding them through the woods; seldom did they ever see a formal gallop, but they won races.

At the time of the first lambing, we were preparing four for the spring season, T's old schoolmaster Log; Heidi (Ebnal Goddess); Roman Receipt (nicknamed Romeo), and the old man of the party, Rough Scot.

The small farm cottage at Frant housed Margaret's farm manager/groom/ general help, a 'salt of the earth' man called George Adams. He knew nothing of horses when he had arrived but by the end he knew much and became devoted not only to his boss but also to our sport. Point-to-pointing for me was all-consuming – until our first lambing came along, that is.

* * *

The sheep were in the fields fully five months before we moved into the cottage, and then into just the bedrooms and kitchen. Altering the old barn to make it ready for sheep had to come before the carpet for the sitting room, and the making of the feed troughs before knocking out the fireplace. First there was hay to be made. Hateful stuff! Not for me romantic notions of lolling on top of a cart-load, wisp in mouth, eyes gazing up at clear blue sky, or drinking gallons of cider while humping bales into stooks. Hay fever, twine cuts and, should the weather actually be sunny leading to shorts being worn, prickly rash saw to that.

'We'll start on the cottage after the hay is in,' T promised.

After the hay we started the straw, bought off a local farmer after he had combined his crop.

And it rained. For days. Straw was ruined. Much of the hay was, too. I attempted a start on the garden – at least it was soft ground to dig – and planted some wallflowers around the cottage, their wobbly stems waving tremulously about four inches above the wet ground.

In the night a few of the sheep escaped into the garden and ate every one of them.

* * *

Every time I asked T what he would like for his birthday the answer was the same: a tractor. He knew, of course, that I could not possibly buy one.

Then, inspiration! Perhaps he *could* have what he wanted. So, a rare visit to the local town was made, to a shop well remembered from childhood. It was well stocked, and even seemed to smell the same, and soon I became engrossed in all on show, with many new ideas and models as well as some old favourites still going strong. I turned over a weird-looking Womble (it was well before the days of play stations and x-boxes), picked up a cuddly teddy bear, admired a handsome rocking horse and then, seeing in the furthest corner a model farmyard, I hastened over, just as a young salesman approached.

'Can I help you?' he enquired.

'Well, I'm looking for a tractor actually.'

'Well now, here's one that can be ridden by a toddler, or there are some smaller models over here.'

He led the way to them. As I pondered, the salesman, seeking to assist, asked politely, 'For what *age* do you want it, Madam?'

Somehow, I managed to keep a straight face but confess I did not have the courage to tell the truth. In the end I chose a model tractor, and then added to it a sheep, three lambs, a collie, a turkey and a horse and rider, representing our farm in perfect plastic detail.

T's face was a picture when he opened the parcel, each item carefully packaged.

'I chose three lambs because you said you wanted two- or three-lamb ewes, and presumably the more lambs we have the better.'

'Well, you're right about the last part, but two-or three-lamb ewes means ewes that have already been breeding for two or three years.'

There was still plenty to learn where sheep were concerned and so I determined to find out more. This was years before the internet and the world wide web with its instant information, to say nothing of Wikipedia. Instead, I tried the Encyclopaedia Britannica. That tome filled me with important facts and figures from around the world none of which, it seemed, bore the remotest sign of help to a housewife cum local reporter in Sussex struggling to learn how to look after sheep. More practical hints came from various MAFF leaflets. From reading them I could drop casual remarks such as, 'I suppose we'll be separating ewes with twin lambs from those with singles to give the doubles better grazing, will we?'

And, 'We'd better make sure we give them enough food before lambing to avoid twin lamb disease, this pregnancy toxaemia sounds terrible.'

* * *

In the outside world, Ross McWhirter was killed by the IRA outside his London home, believed to be because he was offering financial rewards to IRA informers. With his twin brother, Norris, the pair founded the Guinness Book of Records, still known and eagerly anticipated annually throughout the world.

The farm animals for T's birthday may have been plastic, but the line-up was for real another time – and could have cost me my job.

VI

A Porcine Pink Profile

'No! No way!'

'No-one'll know,' T coaxed.

'I'll get the sack.'

Used to some outlandish schemes I might be, such as the time he suggested we should get a milch cow. And who would be left doing the milking twice a day, in addition to shepherding, feeding orphan lambs, working on the local paper, cooking and occasionally doing the housework?

Luckily, that one got binned quickly. This was far more serious. His face told me I wasn't going to win. He had the keys in his hand. It wasn't just that he was going to 'borrow' my new newspaper van, it was what he was going to put in it.

'T, you can't.'

But he was gone.

Suddenly, he bounced back in, charged up the stairs two at a time, returned a few moments later and without saying a word disappeared again, but not before I'd seen what he was wearing. What an apparition. Dark glasses were customary but a wig! My wig, with long flowing hair as was then fashionable.

It was all to do with a request from the BBC. They were making a documentary about factory farming. Our task was to provide a representative of various farm animals. The idea was then to place them in an orderly line across a field. As if!

Most were easily procured: a horse, of course; the sheep and the turkey were equally easy and my mother still had a few cattle so a jet-black

Aberdeen Angus posed no problem, either. A solitary hen was provided from somewhere and a neighbour obliged with a goat. But a pig. There wasn't one nearby.

At last T located one some distance away and he'd seconded my van to fetch it.

Apart from the obvious smell and mess the pig made, it also began rooting underneath the driver's seat so tilting it forward and pushing T almost into the windscreen.

To this day I don't know if anyone spotted the long-haired 'female' driving my van with a distinctly porcine pink face resting on 'her' shoulder as 'she' drove along.

At least this pig was alive, unlike the shock I received after work one day when, looking forward to a bath I found it was already occupied – by the carcass of a pig. T had brought one home from an abattoir and deposited it in the bath until such time as he decided to cut it into joints for the freezer.

The long-haired 'female' driving with a distinctly porcine pink face resting on 'her' shoulder

* * *

Apart from a tractor we also needed a lorry, both for farm work and for carrying horses. The idea was to buy a flatbed vehicle for transporting hay and straw, and a removeable container so that, when fitted, it could double up as a horsebox or, with the separate sheep decks also to be made, as a conveyor for them. T acquired a flatbed quite easily, then set about finding the container.

One breakfast, as he scoured the advertisements in the *Farmers Weekly,* he said casually, 'I think we might go to Scotland for the container.'

'Oh, yes,' I laughed, then looked up and saw that he meant it.

Even allowing for four days and three nights away it was going to be the cheapest option.

After a conversation with the Scotsman, whose accent was nearly unintelligible to my southern ears I gleaned enough to gather that it could indeed be built for us. A few days later a photograph of father and son proudly standing beside one of their hand-crafted containers arrived, and we agreed a deal. Three weeks and it would be ready, and would we please bring them up a ton of straw, as it was in short supply up there.

After about four weeks, and well into November, we were assured the container would be ready by the week-end. We remembered the ton of straw – loaded with curses by T and Tim, but what a blessing it was to prove – squeezed a suitcase between the bales, covered it all with a tarpaulin and piled into the lorry: T at the wheel drumming his fingers impatient to be off, Tim in the passenger seat, myself in the gap between the two that felt like a couple of inches, and our two dogs on the ledge behind us. Roddy, the black Labrador gundog had a wise, old-fashioned broad head and Nicky, whose black Labrador-type coat gave way to a tell-tale white chest and muzzle indicated the collie in him.

Nicky, left, and Roddy, faithful companions.

Nicky had been born one Christmas; his siblings were the pale cream of their mother, a Labrador, but Nicky was more like the working sheepdog of his errant father who had called at the home of his mother uninvited. Named after St Nicholas, he had much more of the nervous collie character. I brought him with me into the marriage and he was a precious part of my life for 14 years. I had given Roddy (Nimrod) to T as a surprise birthday present one year.

They were surrounded by tins of dog food bought at the last minute and not their usual brand, and our extra sweaters, which were to prove another blessing.

With a throaty roar the engine burst into life and with a hiss of the air-brakes we were off, heading for London, the M1, M6, and up to the Grampians near Aberdeen in Bonnie Scotland; the M25 was then in the early stages of construction and it was through central London that we had to drive.

When we stopped at a caff on the M1 our vehicle was dwarfed by the huge articulated and giant continental lorries hemming us in. Ours looked child's play by comparison so, having often driven a Land Rover and trailer with horses on board I climbed confidently into the driver's seat. This was too far away from the steering wheel which itself was too wide; neither was the vehicle power assisted, and it felt heavy and strangely different. Unperturbed, I started up and turned on to the motorway, and soon mastered the hang of it – or thought I had. That changed when I tried to pass a seemingly-endless car transporter. Inch by careful inch we crept alongside until its length blocked my left side and the crash barrier my right. Suddenly, I felt overcome by claustrophobia. A puff of wind, it seemed, would send me off course as nervously I clenched the wheel, my knuckles white, concentration springing on a headache. We were half way past, at the point of no return and beads of cold sweat broke out all over my body. It seemed more than I could manage, but somehow, I **had** to get by. Other drivers hounded me on my tail. The transporter maintained its steady pace, just a little slower than ours, and I lost count of how many of its load of cars in line we had passed for they were all the same size, colour and shape. Finally, we got by that wretched vehicle and blood drained from my head in relief as a faint voice which I barely recognised as my own spluttered, 'T, I don't feel well.'

Weakly I indicated left and T helped me steer the lorry on to the hard shoulder where thankfully it came gently to a halt. As I gulped in refreshing drafts of blessed fresh air, a roaring noise heralded the transporter trundling by.

Gretna Green at dusk was our first glimpse of Scotland but what a plain, **un**romantic place it seemed. The warmth of a cosy bed and breakfast contrasted with the bitter, sub-zero temperature outside, and the cheerful widow land-lady insisted that the dogs should be allowed inside.

Plans for an early start next day were thwarted when we discovered the lorry's water hose had broken. Tim and T disappeared back over the border to Carlisle in search of the part with promises that we would be well on our way by lunch. By tea-time with the wintry night drawing in and a radio bulletin warning of a bad accident on the Carlisle road, alarm set in. Leaving the bright coal fire, I hurried down the road to the local police station, the two dogs at my side.

'Gone looking for a part, you say?' the copper eyed me suspiciously. 'Have you had a tiff, or has he gone off with a lady friend?'

Patiently, I explained that we hadn't had a row and anyway his teenage son was with him. The look on his face told me he didn't rule out two men looking for a 'part.' Clearly, working from Gretna Green had imbued him with such cynicism.

It was not far back to the B&B, clenching my hands inside woollen gloves to try and warm them, and just as we reached it, I heard the welcome roar of the lorry. The kindly landlady insisted on giving us a high tea, refusing payment for it, and then, with dusk closing in and the first snow-flakes falling, we set off.

Within half an hour the snow became a blizzard, large flakes settling and quickly covering the ground, the landscape already blacked out by nightfall. Conditions became worse when the heater on the driver's side packed up and even with the wipers working overtime it could not clear the glass. Improvisation swiftly followed when we disconnected the passenger's heater hose and Tim and I took turns to hold it up, until we found some binder twine and tied it into its new position, directing its blast to the driver's screen, leaving a small cleared patch through which T could peer at the rapidly deteriorating road ahead.

By now, only a narrow width of road was passable and already many vehicles were abandoned. When fog came down to compound difficulties, we were close to giving up, but we made it to a small hotel in Forfar, helped by the ton of straw which had weighted us down at the back and prevented the lorry from spinning on the treacherous road.

We set out next morning in better conditions for the last leg to take us into the foothills of the Grampians, sunshine glistening on the snow-clad countryside. When a car screeched towards us, we dismissed its driver as a maniac. Suddenly, two more followed, swerving wildly across the single-track road while T slammed on the brakes and sounded the lorry's foghorn of a hooter.

I turned on the radio, more to calm my jangled nerves than anything. 'Now, to bring us up to date with the progress of the RAC rally on the mountain section of snowbound Scotland, we go over to…'

So that was it – and what's more we earned ourselves a quid by towing one of the luckless contestant's cars out of a ditch.

At length we crossed a stone bridge over a sparkling river then climbed, twisting higher and higher to the coniferous forests and occasional rocky outcrop surrounded by heather. Swerving to avoid another rally car, we pulled into a muddy driveway, a collie bitch rushing out in frenzied greeting. There below us, in a sea of mud and slush, was the farmstead and in we trundled.

Our new container, under a makeshift cover, was being worked on by father and son with primitive equipment. A plump, jovial woman greeted us from the grey stone house, apron tied around her ample middle, scarf wound around her head.

'C'mon in, they'll be ready in a minute or two, they're just doing the finishing touches. I've some home-killed beef in the oven for 'ee.'

We glanced at each other as she stalled for time for her menfolk, but who could resist her welcome anyway.

First, I took the dogs for a walk up the mountain. It was glorious and the crisp air invigorating. I set my sights on a lone, leafless tree, its outline bent nearly horizontal after years of straining against the prevailing wind. We ploughed through the snow, the dogs bounded over the protruding clumps of heather, and we circled back just in time to find all hands-on deck. The four available men, two pairs of father and son, manhandled the container on to the lorry; they stood back and we held our collective breaths: it fitted perfectly.

Inside, the house was warm and the beef welcome. There seemed to be television sets in every room, but a trip to the loo meant slipping across the snowy back yard to a small, unlit hut housing an Elsan.

We set off feeling well-fed, something we were to find the dogs did, too. T took the wheel, Tim and I snuggled into our seats and the dogs curled up on the ledge behind us. After a few miles it did not seem so cosy. A loud bang like the lorry backfiring was swiftly followed by a nauseous smell of gas. A few moments later it happened again, surrounding us in an unpleasant fug. If it was that close it couldn't be the lorry. Tim and I glanced at each other and then behind us. It was Roddy. He was farting so frequently in our confined space that we had to lower the window every few minutes no matter how cold it was outside. We cursed that new dog food and coined the phrase that lasted down the years of 'doing a Roddy.'

The long drive to Aberdeen to collect the container for the lorry. A cramped cab for five of us but a memorable journey.

Doing a "Roddy"

Instead of bypassing Edinburgh, we drove into the centre and parked our newly-resplendent lorry in Princes Street, beneath the magnificent castle, and gave ourselves a brief tour round.

That night, spent in a B&B on the hillside of Jedburgh, its attractive stone houses overlooking the river winding its way round the fine old church below, we relaxed. Driving on over the Border country next morning, patches of snow were still around. We travelled mile upon deserted mile uphill and down dale occasionally passing through a sleepy village, the landscape in between dotted with sheep. It was desolate but beautiful, tranquil countryside.

'We'll need some diesel before long,' T remarked as he passed a filling station at full speed.

'You've just missed one.'

'That's only got single stamps.' It was the era of Green Shield stamps, which when stuck into several books could be exchanged for goods from a catalogue or in store. Eventually, it morphed into Argos.

More miles slipped by until at length another fuel station loomed. T's jaw was set firmly and, anticipating my cry, said with poker face, 'That's only got double stamps. There's a town soon and we're bound to do better there.'

The fuel gauge was now firmly set on E. Was it E for 'empty' or E for 'enough'? Somehow, we made it to the next town. We found diesel all right – but no stamps. There was nothing for it but to fill up.

Was it E for empty or E for enough?

Some few hours later, as we crawled bumper to bumper in the clogged-up atmosphere and snarling hum of London on the last but most tedious leg of the journey home we knew which part of our travels we preferred.

* * *

By Christmas, the cottage was just about ready for habitation. I had wallpapered our little bedroom – a bold and large coloured pattern that would make one cringe today, but was obviously liked then. At length, I pasted the last brush of glue, pressed the paper against it and smoothed out any air bubbles with my hands, and stood back; definitely couldn't see any blemishes!

As the sheep had become Houdini experts, it would help to be living on site, for they delighted in finding new ways of getting out of, around, under, and sometimes even over 'sheep-proof' fencing.

Being Christmas, it was also turkey time. T used to rear about 300 and I soon discovered that they are only likeable as day old chicks when they are sweet, fluffy, chirpy little things. By the next day they are already unpleasant birds, intent on cannibalism, feather-pecking and gouging out the contents of each other's backsides; after that they try and pick out each other's eyes unless they have been de-beaked, as well as being susceptible to every ailment going.

Come December, trips for Christmas shopping were scant because the turkey trade took precedence, with all the neck-wringing, plucking, drawing and hanging, followed by dressing for the oven and delivery to all the individual customers, work that took us late into the evening and early hours and meant Christmas parties could be attended only in the imagination. The best day of all is when the turkeys take pride of place on Christmas dinner plates.

Before all that, my main job, apart from feeding the turkeys daily, was to take orders for them – many of which came from Courier staff via Bella and her tea trolley – and then spend the days leading up to Christmas in delivering them.

Not the way I would normally check the turkeys – but this is how the Kent & Sussex Courier photographer wanted it!

The turkeys were housed in the long shed at Frant which originally had been a small dairy. When Margaret took it on, she had, first, black Aberdeen Angus cattle which soon showed they could escape even the redoubtable efforts of George Adams to keep them penned in. Her next venture was into hens, and the barn was kitted out with expensively-made wooden slats. It didn't seem to take too long to fail and it was empty by the time T and his turkeys came along. It seemed perfect – until one night a fox jumped about four feet up to and through a small section of broken window pane. The turkeys by this time were not far off ready for Christmas. The fox killed four, biting them across their throats, taking one for himself and leaving the other three strewn on the floor. But of the remainder, only about half survived because in their panic they had crammed against the far wall and those at the front were suffocated by the rest (as was to happen so tragically and far more seriously to spectators at the Hillsborough football ground in April 1989.)

We had to let a lot of people down for their turkeys that year – and most of our annual holiday fund was wiped out, too.

Our move was into just some of the cottage. Stepping across the draughty floorboards of the bare sitting room and wondering how to get used to the clatter of the generator, we reached for a celebratory drink.

The days when water was drawn from the garden well were gone; instead, water was piped from the nearby ancestral seat, Bayham Abbey. Nor, we hoped, were the new incumbents likely to meet the fate of the gamekeeper who had lived there until he met a poacher's bullet. Back in 1654 Newlands Cottage had been lived in by a Mr Porter, pre-dating when the Bayham Estate, headed by Earl (John Jeffrey Pratt) Camden had bought Great Shoesmiths from a Mr Egles in the 18th century.

Soon we learnt about the generator's quirky temperament. Cranking her into life resulted in hands and clothes being smothered in black oil. Sparks literally flew every time she started up, giving a series of hiccups, and the lights inside the cottage flickered menacingly. She stubbornly refused to turn off automatically although T eventually persuaded her to start at the touch of a switch. She made us feel rather smug every time there was a power cut – it was shortly after the era of the three-day week – until she went on strike herself when we quickly reverted to hurricane lamps and candles. Once under full steam the generator chugged steadily for an hour or two, then apparently paused for breath, caught it, and surged on again until time for lights out. Our nearest neighbours, half a mile away, told us they always knew what time we went to bed.

Cranking the quirky generator into life resulted in hands and clothes being smothered in black oil.

When T fitted a silencer there was a marginal improvement, and then, just as he had to be away for a couple of days, he announced proudly that he had fully automated her (all this was just five miles from the commuter town of Tunbridge Wells in affluent south-east England, in the mid-1970s). It was a cold winter night and I went to bed with overcoat and hurricane lamp nearby. With the last light turned off, the generator's chug duly got less and less, and slower and slower until there was blissful silence. He had done it! Snuggling down, pulling bedclothes over my ears, I was almost asleep when I was sure there were slow chug-chug sounds. Must be dreaming. Splatter. Splurt. Seconds later, the generator steamed into full force evidently up for a fight every bit as determined as the Cod War currently waging in the North Sea between Britain and Iceland. There was nothing for it but to spring wearily (if that's possible) into my coat, fumble for the matches, grope down the stairs, unlock the back door, trip over the loose paving bricks, unlock the garage door, and flick the wretched switch up – and then wait a freezing eternity to check she really did slow down and turn right off before another demon turned her head.

We had been in the cottage little over a month when my parents asked us to house-sit at The Mast Head while they went away for a week-end. It was only three miles away so we were happy to oblige as it was easy to pop back to the farm. The first thing I noticed on my return home next morning was our farm gate hanging open; we were meticulous about keeping it shut because of the dogs. Then I saw it. A smashed window. Hands fumbling, I unlocked the door. At once it was apparent that some nick-knacks and a couple of racing trophies had disappeared from the living room. I raced up the steep, narrow stairs two at a time. T's watch, left to him by his father, had gone from the mantlepiece. Every drawer in our bedroom chest had been rifled and left open but they had found nothing of value there. Had they but known, they only had to look under the last layer of shirts in the bottom drawer to find a substantial wad of notes that T had stashed there.

"Has she ever ridden before?"

Spring, officially at least, was approaching, and soon we would fetch home a number of ewes that had been out at winter keep, in readiness for lambing. Not all had gone well; one ewe had eaten rhododendron and died; another couple had managed to get drowned. But, alas, something unforeseeable happened which was to have worse results. One batch of sheep that were away were attacked by two dogs, just when the unborn lambs were at their most vulnerable. The dogs ran riot in their field, chasing the ewes, catching a couple by the hind leg and worrying them so much that the alarmed ewes fled towards the fence, throwing themselves against it, struggling to find a way through. It was shambles. The weight of the ewes at the back pressed on those in front, eventually forcing the fencing to give way so that they piled through, trampling over the unfortunate ones who had been pinned down in front. Frantically they struggled to their feet, shook their heads, found their trembling legs and staggered after their mates streaming down the road. Their momentum increased until they were at full gallop, twisting and turning down the narrow lanes. Eventually they swung through an open gateway into a field but the damage was done, as we were to discover during lambing.

Another occasion was amusing rather than serious. We had been to a smart wedding and were dressed accordingly when we decided to take a turn by some of our sheep out at keep. We looked an incongruous pair climbing over the gate, T in his best suit and white shirt, me in pretty dress and high heels. At first all seemed well and we were about to leave. But there, on the far side of the flock, was a ewe with a prolapse. This, I was to learn, was a fairly common problem approaching lambing time caused by a ewe pushing her vagina out of her vulva, possibly because of the growing lamb(s) inside her. It was a dark, pinky red mass the size of something between a tennis ball and a melon.

It was relatively easy to push back inside – once she was caught. And high heels were definitely not the gear in which to try and corner a ewe, nor T's smart suit ideal for wearing when turning over and operating on the ewe once caught; he gently pushed the mass back inside her, and hoped that would last as we had no T-shaped gadget designed to keep the 'ball' inside her. We straightened up to head back – and found we had attracted an audience of the nearby council house occupiers peering at our efforts over the fence.

It was clothes of a different hue the day T went to collect the lorry from a servicing.

It was in a garage in Tonbridge so to collect it back I agreed to drop T off at Wadhurst Station, just two stops away from Tonbridge. A train was in the station, so he slammed the car door and sprinted towards it. He grabbed a seat just as the doors were closing. A few minutes later the train whizzed past Tunbridge Wells Central, followed by the big Tonbridge station, and then Sevenoaks – and did not stop until it reached Charing Cross. This was not the only problem. T was dressed in muddy gumboots and waterproof trousers and his crumpled jacket was held together by binder twine round his middle. The whole ensemble smelled distinctly of sheep. Every other passenger on that train, male or female, wore a dark suit and carried a briefcase.

This was not his only difficulty. When he alighted in London to look for a return train, T also realised he had no money. And suddenly, there also walking up the platform on her way to meet an editor, perhaps, was my mother, and she only too happy to oblige with enough cash to get him home!

* * *

In late March, a few weeks after Margaret Thatcher became leader of the Conservative party, followed just two days later by the coal-miners accepting a 35% pay rise from the Labour government, it was freezing hard. Our first lambing was due to start, and that was when we decided to drive the flock into the warmth of the barn. By the time we had coaxed them inside on that bitterly cold spring night, it was dusk outside and we returned to the deserted field for a final check that no sheep had been left behind. An owl swirled past in the gloaming and above stars twinkled brightly, indicating another sharp frost approaching. I clenched my fingers inside my gloves trying to get the circulation going again while underfoot our boots made a clear crunch on the remains of snow crystallised by frost. Tim had arrived home from college and joined me on the trek.

'What's that?' he called.

It looked like another patch of snow, tucked into the north-facing bank, but it seemed to move. Must be the wind. We peered closer.

It was a lamb! The mite, only a few hours old, had crept under the barbed wired fence into the thorn hedge and could not get back. Tim tucked it inside his windcheater, his gangly teenage hands now gentle as he cradled it.

It was our first, all-important lamb, and we called him Tiny. Our future viability depended on a good initial lambing crop, to service those agricultural mortgage repayments we had so boldly undertaken in return for our dream come true to go into farming.

The lamb bleated plaintively as we traipsed to the barn. Its mother had long since abandoned it and to try and find her in the seething morass of panting ewes in the barn would be impossible. Instead, we laid it in some hay the other side of the fence partition from the ewes. It was remarkably strong, with round, innocent eyes and curly coat, and he drank well from the bottle of made-up milk we brought down. Tiny was our first 'suck' or 'cade' lamb, though little did we guess then what a part orphan lambs were to play that first year. The snow lay thickly for three days dispelling belief that it would last no more than a few hours so late in the year.

It was freakish then, but no words exist for what followed; if they did, they would be as stinging as the bitter cold and rain.

No more of the ewes panting in the barn looked like lambing imminently, so we walked back up the track to the cottage, through the cold rooms until we reached the welcome warmth of the kitchen where the Rayburn churned out a glowing heat; there we hung our gloves and jackets. We prepared for racing next day, Easter Saturday, discussing prospects over steaming mugs of tea. That spring the point-to-points we loved were to provide us with our only brief breaks from the lambing field, when the meetings themselves did not fall victim to the weather. The local one was already cancelled, but the weather in East Anglia was better. I thought back to my early point-to-point wins.

* * *

The first was shortly after I embarked on my time at the Courier in 1968. We started off in a 20-runner field at Tweseldown, near Aldershot, where although we finished sixth, we were only beaten nine lengths. Back there next time, again with 20 runners, we set off in the lead; the new, fit, healthy Tarka was strong, bold, eager and keen beneath me. Nothing, I swear, would have beaten him that day and as we headed out on the second circuit his lead increased. Suddenly, as we approached the next fence, a loose horse swerved across us, taking us with him. In one swift swipe we were out of the race, helpless puppets (just as was to happen to A.P. McCoy in the 2005 Grand National when leading approaching the second Becher's on Clan Royal.) My first reaction was to turn and re-join. Not a hope; the track was too narrow for turning, and Tarka was anyway unstoppable.

My 21st birthday came and went – an oil painting of me racing on Tarka from my parents, a smart sheepskin coat from T, and a slap-up night out for family and friends at Quaglinos in London.

Then off we traipsed to the Surrey Union point-to-point at Tismans, Rudgwick. There were nine runners in the ladies including good horses like Garnett Boy and Young Friendly. But to Tarka there was only one horse in the race. He drew steadily further and further ahead and won by a distance. After three years of trying, suddenly it had been so easy!

After nearly three seasons and numerous second placings, including by a short-head, Tarkaotter suddenly made it all seem so easy. The Surrey Union ladies race at Tismans, Rudgwick, 1968.

Next time out my inexperience lost the day. I brought Tarka through too quickly when there were still three fences to go. I could have made up ground stealthily and still won; as it was, I came too fast, he hit the top of the fence and I shot out of the saddle like a bullet.

The transformation continued in 1969. I could barely believe how well Tarka was, even better than before. As I exercised him around the hills, through the woods and along the lanes, his neck hard as iron and bulging with muscles he was, in my dreams, a Cheltenham Gold Cup horse. Gone was the old thin self but neither was there fat on him; he was simply fit. I longed for the start of the point-to-point season.

He was pulling my arms out, even when we were on our own. One day, cantering along a forest track we'd used many times before, he kept pulling out more. We were approaching the end of the forest, where the track turned into a narrow path at right angles up an impossibly steep, rough hill littered with rabbit holes; ahead was a width of scrub followed by a barbed wire fence and a line of silver birch trees fencing off a field of cattle.

Desperately I tried to pull him up; there was nowhere to go bar straight ahead and the end was looming; far from recognising his place to stop, Tarka was gaining speed. He galloped straight on, across the scrub and through the fence, leaving me somewhere in the branches overhead.

When I went to the doctor with a cut over my eye, he was not sympathetic. In those days, men wore cloth caps when exercising and us girls generally wore a headscarf. As the doctor stitched the cut, he made it clear that I should have been wearing a hard hat. Tarka got away with superficial scratches.

How often did we have a fine January, only to wake up to snow on the morning of the season's first point-to-point in February? That year it was to be March 1 before we set off for Tweseldown, and for the first time Margaret had three runners. Master Jock was in the men's Players Gold Leaf Open (the qualifier for the end-of-season hunter chase championship); Patsy was having her first ride in a race on the now 14-year-old Chasewood in the Ladies, along with me on Tarka. On the morning of a race my dreams of winning invariably turned to a simple, 'please can we both get round ok'. And it was a family joke that we would always have at least one 'pit stop' for me enroute. This time there was Patsy to think about, too.

Tweseldown was in its heyday, with several meetings per season; it was the early meetings that drew the runners, before many other areas of the country had got going. The course enjoyed a springy peat surface that was a joy to ride over and I think the only time it was ever cancelled, bar for thick snow, was if the water jump was flooded because there was not sufficient room beside it to be bypassed. Originally Tweseldown had been one of dozens of 'bona fide' courses scattered throughout the country, run by and for the Army, and was therefore one of very few point-to-point meetings to benefit from permanent buildings; Cottenham in Suffolk was another. We had a wonderful, very large lady valet looking after us and she, plus the lady on the South-East circuit, played an unsung but very helpful role behind the scenes, calming nerves here, fetching an elastic band there, churning out the tea, and keeping an eye on belongings.

Tweseldown retained its original grandstand which would have been splendid for viewing had there not been a high mound on the opposite side of the course, topped by a turret used by the commentator, effectively blocking the view of two thirds of the course. An underground passage linked one side of the course to the other and most spectators used this, and then ran around the mound, twice, during the course of the race to best follow the runners. In 2013 Tweseldown closed as a racecourse, and the area is now used for eventing.

The meeting began well for us when Master Jock finished third, only being collared after the last. Then it was our turn. There were only nine runners. I don't know how Patsy and I ended up being beside each other at the start but with two experienced horses it should not have mattered. But somehow or other we collided in mid-air over the first. That was it, I was gone, knocked out of the saddle and lying rolled up in a ball on the ground. Dismayed.

It was from beside that fence that I cheered Patsy over it when the runners came round again. She pulled up at the 16th for a highly satisfactory initial ride on the perfect schoolmaster. He was by the same sire (Lancewood) as Tarkaotter, and he had given Margaret her first winner a few years earlier at the Old Surrey and Burstow with Guy Peate in the saddle.

Incredibly, another extraordinary thing was to happen to us at Tweseldown two years later. Again, Patsy and I were both in the same race. It was still five years before the law change that would allow us to contend 'men's' races, so we tried wherever possible to race on alternate weeks but sometimes, if a meeting had been cancelled for instance, a clash became unavoidable. So, there were two riders to be weighed out, two horses to be saddled up, and quite possibly not enough help. Whatever the reason, Patsy's horse was delayed coming into the paddock, and the rest of us were about to file out. Under the rules, all her horse had to do was one turn of the parade ring but the officious Army gentleman in charge of proceedings was having none of it. I could hear Patsy's pleadings as I left the paddock. Down at the start I waited for her to come. Nothing. The starter called us into line. She had been prevented from running.

The upshot of this was that Margaret wrote a letter of complaint to the Jockey Club. Next thing was, she was hauled up before the Stewards in Portman Square, London, not something I guess she'd reckoned on. Portman Square is 'hallowed' ground, filled with antique furniture and fine oil paintings of famous horses from the past. To be called there for an enquiry generally spells trouble, although since the late 1960s, defendants had at least been allowed legal representation.

I wish I could ask Margaret now about that day, but basically, she felt she'd been wronged (a fine for being late into the paddock would have been more palatable). The Army official was also at the enquiry and the Stewards listened to both sides of the story. The outcome was that the point-to-point organisers were ordered to return Margaret her entry fee of £5.

Returning to 1969, I had now had the runaway fall at home and the first fence fall at Tweseldown. My nerves were wrecked! It was decided that, in spite of the distance, we would journey all the way down to the Wilton point-to-point, 125 miles away at Badbury Rings, a beauty spot near Blandford Forum in Dorset, the following week.

Tarka never was a good traveller. Halfway there a motorist flagged us down.

'Your trailer's on fire,' he informed us.

We rushed out to the back of the trailer. There, we quickly saw the cause of his concern: the well-intentioned driver had mistaken the steam from Tarka's sweating for smoke.

The journey was down the length of the A272, from East Sussex through West Sussex to the Hampshire border, an A road so well known for its awfulness that there was once a full-length book written about it. Pretty and historical though the points along it are, it was, and doubtless still is, narrow, twisting, and bears little resemblance to a trunk road. Swaying around its bends in a rattling old trailer was not good therapy for Tarka. For drivers of cars stuck in queues behind us, hernias were at a premium. The roads through Hampshire and on into Dorset were not much better.

At length we arrived. Tarka had sweated away his newfound bloom and nearly resembled the hat-rack of old. All we hoped was that we could get round safely.

* * *

Badbury Rings is an iron-age hill fort, now run by the National Trust. The cars for the point-to-point are parked on top of a bank giving spectators a natural grandstand from which to view the races. There were ten runners in the ladies including one of the country's leading horses, the hot favourite Darnick Tower, a chestnut ridden by Mrs Ann Harden; others were Gay Quadrille, Vulganique and Five Aces. Being so far out of my country meant I knew few of the other riders but there was the usual mix of camaraderie and quietness in the ladies changing tent.

As I was legged on to Tarka I sensed nothing of imminent drama, for the feel of the horse beneath me as always banished the nerves. At first when I gathered the reins to canter to the start his rhythm gave me the usual confidence; he gained momentum a little and then, as we headed down the bank – whoosh! He was gone! And this time I couldn't even fight for control because my legs had turned to jelly. My mouth was dry, my arms useless as faster and faster he went. The one good thing about the Badbury Rings course was that it is set in a vast square, with no hedges, trees or other impediments in the infield. And I still had steering, my feeble cry for 'help' being as much use as the wet rag I felt like. I turned him in a huge circle and pointed him back at the other runners now circling patiently at the start. Beyond was a gapless line of tall trees that not even Tarka could take on. Reaching the other runners, he stopped dead. Inevitably, involuntarily, helplessly, I fell off like a sack of potatoes. Plop.

"Has she ever ridden before?" I heard the starter enquire.

The ambulance arrived.

A Land Rover bearing Margaret, T and Patsy arrived. The starter wanted to get the race under way without me.

'No', I protested, 'I'm fine.'

Precious minutes were secured in which to regain my breath and semi-compose myself as the huntsman galloped to retrieve my crash cap which was fast disappearing in the Land Rover.

'Just jump one fence and pull up,' Patsy advised, holding us behind the other runners, and then, with me feeling like a wilting flower in a desert, the race began.

Tarka quickly showed his disdain for such tactics, caught hold of the bit and surged forward, only to have his runaway ideas thwarted by a close-packed line of bobbing equine bottoms.

Jump one fence, be damned! No matter how tightly I held him he succeeded in weaving his way through so that by the third fence he was leading.

There he stayed. Still, I had a close hold of him. Round that tight, tight turn I fear for his legs but he is so full of power that nothing will stop him. One circuit is now completed and we're facing down that hill once more. He lowers his neck. His stride lengthens. His momentum increases. For an instant I get that sinking feeling of being runaway with again but this time I **have** to keep control… the ground levels out and we head out on the final circuit. The whole way round it is the same story. Power. Speed. Superlative jumping. At last, the final fence flicks beneath us and finally I'm able to ease the reins a notch and let him gallop to the line, to a momentous victory. The favourite never got a look in! His rider was the first to congratulate me. Everyone made us welcome, and joined in the celebrations. We had arrived not knowing a soul, with the simple intention of putting two recent falls behind us. We left, after a third fall and an amazing, fairy tale win, feeling we had made new friends.

Tarka was 12 years old. What he could have achieved had his allergy been remedied in his younger days (and had his dodgy legs held together better) has to remain conjecture, but a top hunter chaser at least is my view. Next time out after Badbury Rings we had a crack at the prestigious Heythrop 3½ mile ladies race and I was led to the start. Hopes were high but although bedded at home on peat, inadvertently there was straw in the trailer; the mucus returned and he was unable to perform. Darnick Tower won the race. Of all the horses I was to ride, Tarka remained the most powerful and, on his day, the best.

But Tarkaotter is not the name most associated with me. The young pretender was waiting in the wings.

No more honest pair of eyes ever looked through a bridle

At the time of our first lambing Tarkaotter was a precious memory, and his successor, my mother's hero and perennial favourite among the south-eastern crowds, Rough Scot, was ageing. He had given me dream rides and for nearly a decade had almost never been out of the first three in ladies' races.

He had not looked like achieving that sort of success originally. To begin with, the vet sent to inspect him for pre-purchase soundness declared, 'He'll never stand hunting, let alone racing,' diagnosing spavins (bony growths on the hocks). He apparently then said, 'But I tell you what, I have just the horse for you at home, bound to win you a race.'

The vet stood back from the chunky little iron grey, pointed to the spavined hocks, and addressed Margaret, a woman who loved her racing while knowing very little about horses.

It was her colours that she loved to see around the local tracks. Later, it was her daughters wearing them that brought her the greatest pleasures – and heartaches.

The vendor, Peggy Pacey, who also bred the little horse, was nearly 80. A beret sat askew her head above a leathery, lined face. She held the lead rope, silently willing the vet to pass him. Hadn't this hoss been the very divil to break? Buck, buck, buck. Hadn't she at one time aimed him in long reins at the iron rails more than 4ft 6ins high to surely break his neck? Little devil had cleared them, reins trailing behind.

Margaret and her advisor, Guy Peate, whispered.

He said, "Well, you pay a vet to take his advice…"

A small smile turned up the sides of Margaret's mouth. "To listen to his advice, may be… But I like him, I like his colour."

She turned to Peggy.

"£400."

"Deal done," Peggy spat into her palm and grasped the younger woman's hand. Margaret already had the youngster's winning older full brother Master Jock (by Jock Scot out of Greenstone) for whom, when he was just broken, she had paid the then considerable sum of £1,000. He was much more what a racehorse should look like.

It was more than hocks that were wrong with Rough Scot, as he was named, and it was more than temperament. He was small, plain, and he couldn't walk to save his life.

Yet no more honest pair of eyes ever looked through a bridle. An iron grey (nearly black as a youngster) he stood about 16 hands and looked more like a hunter than a thoroughbred racehorse, with deep chest, stocky front legs and plenty of heart room – oh, that heart.

No more honest pair of eyes ever looked through a bridle, Photo Jim Meads

Rough Scot at Melton

Rough Scot was nearly black as a youngster, and almost white in old age

He was never going to be a great horse but that he was such a good one – winning 16 races and placing 30 times in a point-to-point career spanning ten years and 60 races – was in itself remarkable.

* * *

Driving to point-to-points with a horse and trailer behind was not always straight forward.

'You're mad,' father said for the umpteenth time as we set about stowing picnic, saddle, kitbag and all the usual point-to-point paraphernalia into the Land Rover, snatching a quick cup of coffee as we did so, while he, leisurely, could enjoy breakfast before donning his hunting kit later – much later – in the morning. The South-East point-to-point season did not start until March, and so February meant forays either to Tweseldown in Hampshire, or to East Anglia, in the old, cold, bumpy Land Rover.

It was still quite dark as we drove into the cold February morning with mother safely ensconced in her 'throne', a garden chair wedged over the picnic basket in the back of the Land Rover, a horse blanket wrapped around her, the horse and trailer behind.

London was a formidable barrier for those in the South-East seeking meetings before their own season started, and we always seemed to hit it at the rush hour. We never realised the lack of signposts at strategic points until it came to towing a trailer and finding ourselves on the wrong road with no easy turn back – how do foreigners ever cope?

We did manage a U-turn once, in Regent Street. Somehow, we missed the turning to Vauxhall Bridge and found ourselves travelling northwards up Regent Street. Undaunted, T performed a perfect U-turn. Next, we missed a No Entry sign and gaily drove the wrong way down a one-way street into Trafalgar Square – it was the surprised look on the face of a Rolls Royce chauffer which gave the game away, but by then there was nothing for it but to continue.

It is never too late to see the sights of London, I suppose, and Land Rover and trailer continued, wafting the occasional piece of straw towards surprised Londoners. Eros waved us through Piccadilly Circus and past Downing Street, till Big Ben chimed our way across Westminster Bridge.

Stopping and starting in the usual London jam another day a cheery taxi driver drew alongside and called, 'You've got a flat.' We jacked up the trailer, horse and all, but now we really had cause for concern for another of the trailer wheels already had a slow puncture. With frequent stops for air, we got there safely.

Breaks for petrol, loos or tea were inevitable on these marathon journeys, of course; but a petrol stop was determined not by whether the tank was empty, nor if there was an easy entrance and exit, but (as we have seen for the lorry journey to Aberdeen) only if a suitably high multiplicity of the right coloured stamps were on offer. As for tea, we usually stopped on a motorway and plumped not for the smart end where tea is served in polite plastic thimbles, but for the transport café with good old-fashioned pint mugs.

After struggling through a particularly bad stretch of road we were stopped again.

'Hey, guv, did you know your trailer is on fire?' a worried looking driver asked.

We'd heard this one before, of course, but flew out and duly found that the 'smoke' came from our sweating horse.

There was another night when we got hopelessly lost in Essex – signposts were seldom lit up – and we ended up driving straight over cross-roads into Ford's Dagenham works. We always seemed to make it somehow. There was an air of adventure about our early meetings that to start the season near home would almost have been tame.

But another long drive nearly had drastic results. As usual we had seen to petrol, oil, water and other non-equine needs the previous night, and we left for Norwich at about 8am. But we had quite simply miscalculated the time it would take to get there, and it was not until we stopped for a coffee that we realised time was running short. Driving a horse in a trailer at 50mph is no joke and when we went to overtake an articulated lorry on the A11 there was no room for sway as gradually, inch by inch, we gained on that uncooperative lorry – but at least it was T who was driving. The horse's chance was hardly enhanced by such a drive and, with just a few miles left, we smelt the engine getting hotter and hotter.

We made it, with only five minutes to spare before declaring. With barely time to walk round the paddock and limber up after such a long journey in the trailer it is no surprise that he never got into the race and finished last of four. It was my first ride on Master Jock. There were only five races, two were already run when we got there, and it seemed no time at all before the poor horse, a beaten favourite, was being hauled all that way home again.

But our long outings sometimes ended with success, like that to Badbury Rings, and there was also a never-to-be-forgotten 125-1 double at Moulton, near Newmarket, when Master Jock won the men's open, ridden by David Evatt, and Rough Scot the ladies open (ladies opens had taken the place of ladies adjacents a few years before.) That time a generous father had hired a box for us and all went without a hitch.

Not so the next time. Hunting over, father was persuaded to come pointing. He wanted to take a car in addition to the Land Rover and trailer. 'No, too extravagant,' we dismissed it out of hand.

I was having my second ride on Master Jock, at Marks Tey, Essex, and he was going really well, leading as we approached the last open ditch. He was 'wrong' at it; I slapped him down the shoulder to tell him to take off early – but he ploughed straight on through it, coming down, and bringing down another horse ridden by Jean Oyler. Rough Scot, of course, would simply have put himself right in such a situation.

Picking herself up, Jean said, 'I've broken my collarbone'.

I went to move my arm – and realised I had done so, too.

On the same day Patsy rode at Tweseldown, travelling to different far-flung courses being the only way we could avoid taking each other on; she also had a fall and broke a finger.

I was taken to Chelmsford Hospital, in the town centre, and the horse waited patiently in the car park. It happened to be Grand National day. As I walked in, still wearing racing colours, arm in sling, there were several startled looks from people leaving their shops and offices. Two little boys peered over the back of the trailer and cried, 'Coo, 'oov'e you got in there, Red Alligator?' (1968 winner of the Grand National.)

On the return journey, nursing a broken collar bone for three hours in a bumpy, jarring Land Rover, I wished I could have eaten those earlier words and accepted Dad's offer of bringing a car as well.

Master Jock was unhurt. Like his younger brother, he possessed limbs of iron and never missed a season through leg trouble. He was bigger and better looking than Rough Scot and won an impressive 12 races in his career, several of them Opens.

Rough Scot was not as speedy, but he almost never made a jumping error, being so compact that even at full gallop he could put himself right.

Master Jock, as the pony Mr Linnet before him, eventually went to my brother in Wales where Tim not only enjoyed hunting the old horse with the South Pembrokeshire but also rode in a number of point-to-points, twice winning his hunt members' race. By chance, my brother, sister and I all lived where our local point-to-point was held on Easter Monday and on one memorable occasion, all three of us won our respective hunt races: the South Pembrokeshire (Tim,) the North Cotswold (Patsy,) and the Eridge for me.

Family fun – Siblings Tim, Anne and Patsy Holland with Tim's children, Hannah, Alex and Abigail.

And T, Anne and stepson Tim.

That was long before sheep farming and orphan lambs entered my life.

* * *

To return to that first lamb in 1975, when Tim had found the abandoned mite half hidden by snow in the hedgerow: in the morning there was another covering of snow but steam still poured out of the barn from the overheated flock. At first Tiny was not to be seen, but all was well and he drank readily from the bottle. Luckily no more lambs had been born (they weren't officially due to start for another few days), so we turned out the flock and hurried off to Cambridgeshire, reaching the point-to-point at Cottenham just in time to see one of our horses fall (no harm done), while the other pulled up. Not an auspicious start, but we could only hope for better. Farming was anyway taking precedence over our lives.

We soon discovered we would need a helper keeping an eye on things if we were away at a race-meeting. Luckily, a student son of a local cattle farmer and hop-grower filled in when needed. Similarly, keeping the horses fit and exercised had to be fitted in around the lambing, to say nothing of work. As for keeping ourselves fit, that was soon taken care of, that initial rounding up of the sheep only being the first of many such efforts.

It was two hours or so drive home from Cottenham, straight into wellingtons, and down to the sheep. We decided to bring them in again as more snow was threatened and Tim was there to help us. Before long the flock was following the tempting plastic bag and gathered in the track outside the black barn. But sheep are not so stupid – they remembered the place only too well and did not want to go back there. No amount of cajoling, coaxing, swearing, pushing; shouting, hitting, stamping, running or jumping would persuade them that it was in their own interests on such a cold night to sleep in a snug, warm, barn. Instead, it degenerated into a slanging match.

'I'm sure other sheep farmers don't do it this way.'

No reply.

'I said, I'm sure other…'

'Stop that ewe behind you.'

'Stop it yourself.'

Silence.

'I'm not doing this every night, it's ridiculous.'

No reply.

'We must have a sheepdog.'

'Yell at them.'

'My voice is hoarse, I can't shout any more.'

'You seem to be shouting all right now.'

Still the wretched sheep stood unconcernedly in the track. If we managed to push some forward others darted out behind, swiftly followed by more shouting. My arms felt disassociated from my body as they swung up and down mechanically, every muscle in my body aching, throat dry, and in any moment my legs would most certainly drop off.

Something made us remember there was a light in the barn; we turned it on, its powerful beam flooded the interior and those dear, stupid sheep, surprised and mesmerised, shuffled steadily in. It had taken nearly three hours and it was one-twenty in the morning. We staggered back into the cottage, my weary limbs thinking of nothing but bed.

'What's for supper, Anne?'

* * *

All thoughts of food had long since vanished but it was, on reflection, a long time since the point-to-point picnic at lunch time!

Luckily the Rayburn coughed up a creditable casserole, which we washed down with passable plonk, reviving our flagging spirits and humour, thankful for such medicine all the way up to bed.

The alarm clock shrilled. It seemed impossible, but it was time to get up and go down to the flock and turn them out again. It was Easter Sunday, but church was missed as we tramped the fields where the hungry and pregnant flock roamed, scattered snowflakes on the ground, the trees stark and wintry – anything but spring-like.

Neither was it to be an Easter with dear little lambs skipping around the place looking pretty. Instead, Tiny died. He had nuzzled deep into the hay seeking the maternal warmth and protection he was denied, and he had quite simply suffocated. I felt bitter remorse, but nothing could revive him.

The snow gave way to continuous rain by mid-day and we changed during our brief visits to the cottage for a scrap lunch and snack tea, venturing out with renewed vigour. Admittedly it sapped again quickly, and clothes remained dry only briefly as we looked for ewes in difficulties, traipsing round the fields. In the following weeks, washing-up was saved for once a day. Any disapproving looks were retaliated by assurances, not always subtle, that chores could not be done while tramping round wet fields. Conversation became a relic of the past, necessitated in short, staccato form only when telepathy failed.

Every blade of grass became known personally in the steeply undulating field, the fine oak by the gate acting as a guard. Its leaves were slowly turning a mellow gold hiding the intricate dark brown patterns of the twigs stretched out like lace on the end of its branches. The grass on top of the hill was awash and gave way to a sea of mud around the feeding troughs. In the far corner a gorse bank led to a dell, a sheltered secluded spot where the ewes liked to lamb. A stream normally no more than a trickle raced the far side of the hedge and swirled into the usually silent Chalybeate spring pond, sending ripples across it and startling the moorhens. Our neighbour's field beyond looked like a lake, only a few longer stems of grass protruding through the water. It would be another 26 years before there was a spring as wet, when the foot and mouth pestilence ravaged an unbelieving, shell-shocked countryside.

The far bank, part of Great Shoesmiths, was too steep for agriculture and it swept up to a beech toll, planted by a man in memory of his sons killed in the war; it created a dome that was a landmark for miles around. Underneath lay cool earth with leafy walks, alive with foxes, badgers and grey squirrels. Above were squawking jays, cawing rooks and raucous magpies, their smart plumage disguising their wicked streak. The bank that sloped down to the field by the stream was treeless save for a large beech bough that had fallen from a mighty tree in the toll and finally lay to rest among the brambles and rabbit warrens. Russet-coloured bracken carpeted the bank, its new green yet to unfurl, and golden daffodils flared skywards heralding the coming of spring, their trumpets unaware that spring had receded to winter.

Away from the dell the lower fence ran by our neighbour's hop-garden, a thick, thorny hedge a couple of feet back from the wire offering hundreds of yards of tunnel-like protection to small creatures. The middle of our field stretched in great, sweeping folds, so undulating that sheep could be hidden in pockets unless every yard was scoured. The hill to the gate got positively steeper each time I dragged myself up it, one step forward, two slipping back in the mud. To one side a sunken road, all that remained from the Ironmasters era, lay wet beneath a thin line of thorns.

The rain eased and I sighed in relief when T decided the sheep could stay out for the night. Tim had brought home a girlfriend from college, Jane, and it was to her relief, too, for she had begun to feel she was T's sheepdog as she helped with the rounding up. It was getting dark, time to light the hurricane lamps surrounding the field at intervals which, with flapping plastic bags, were intended to keep foxes away. So, armed with paraffin can and matches, we walked round just once more. The lamps swung gently in the breeze giving a slightly eerie light. The sky cleared, the frost glittered, the stars above twinkled and suddenly we burst into a rendition of *While Shepherds Watched Their Flocks by Night* then laughed. This was Easter, not Christmas!

IX

Defying Gravity

Next day was a drizzling April Fools' Day, the official start to our lambing. Right on cue the lambs began to make their bow into the grey, cheerless world. We set about bringing the new mothers and their offspring in to a long low barn next to the big black barn where we had housed the whole flock those first two nights. This way we could keep them under close surveillance and offer them dry, warm shelter for the first few days before turning them out, the ewes with single lambs into Walnut Tree Field and those with twins into Black Barn Field.

The ewes continued to show their lack of appreciation of our good intentions, so that what should have been five-minute jobs often took half an hour. Most of the ewes were so maternal that they rushed around in dizzy circles as we tried to bring them in but a maddening few spurned their lambs.

I soon became adept at telling the weak lambs from the strong, but to begin with, each was just a slippery, yellow bundle. Walking round I could see a new-born lamb, his mother proudly licking him all over as he lay quite still. The ewe paused for a minute and turned to the grass as if desperate for food to restore her energy after her labours. Suddenly she felt guilty at her own 'greed' and nickered softly to her lamb, not the demanding baa-aa of wanting corn or the full-throated bleat of imminent danger.

She started running away automatically at my approach but stopped in her tracks when she remembered her lamb. She stood staring for a second, as if thinking, 'Now what is the stronger emotion, fear of you or the love of my lamb?'

She strutted back cautiously, bent over her lamb, licked him, cast a sideways glance at me and licked him again as if to make sure he was all right. I stooped to pick him up and she paced back, stamping indignantly. The lamb was too young to run away but he had a healthy kick in him and was quite a weight. As I started to walk up the muddy slope, the mother ran round me in a bleating frenzy. Suddenly she turned away, having lost sight of the lamb in my arms, and trotted frantically this way and that, calling to him urgently. I placed him on the ground for her to see and she ran up, bleating softly.

Picking him up again, progress was even slower, showing her the lamb every few steps as she knocked at my knees; any faster, and she 'lost' him again. Sometimes he bleated back and the ewe came running towards the sound, so before long I was imitating him, and progress was speeded up a little.

Once up at the gate, T cornered the ewe and made what looked like a rugby tackle to floor her; he tossed her over liked a featherweight, ignoring her flailing legs. He sat her up on her haunches, supporting her back and head between his legs and lent over her stomach. From there he cut off the dirty wool around her udder and rear end, then he deftly pulled the teats until a spray of milk shot from each, spurting high into the air. Satisfied the lamb would easily find the milk bar, he next slipped a tight rubber ring over the lamb's tail to dock it and, being a ram lamb, castrated him with a similar ring. In a number of weeks' time, these appendages would simply drop off. He then dabbed iodine on the lamb's navel before putting the pair into the barn.

After a warming mug of tea back at the cottage, we embarked on the evening rounds refreshed. By the time we had dealt with a few more ewes and lambs, fed the rest outside in the troughs, lit the lanterns and got wet again, it was 10 p.m. and once more, we blessed the old Rayburn.

We certainly didn't watch television. If we had, we would have discovered the first episode being aired of a new sit-com called The Good Life – what an irony; comedic was not how I was finding our situation.

And as we struggled through the mud and with the orphans that month who could have guessed that over in New Mexico a 19-year-old by the name of Bill Gates, and his 22-year-old colleague Paul Allen founded a company that was to become known as Microsoft. I was still using a clackety-clack typewriter; my, how the personal computer was to transform our lives, to say nothing of the internet and, crucially, soon after Tim Berners-Lee's world wide web, which came along in embryo form in 1989.

After Peggy Pacey failed to 'break his neck' over iron railings, Rough Scot eventually became biddable enough. But the buck was never completely got out of him; he could pop in a quick one at the end of a day's hunting as readily as at the beginning, and he 'dropped' all of us at the walk. Good horses are meant to have a good walk; 'Scotty's' was abysmal and you'd have to kick him all the way; it was if you fell asleep that he'd whip round and drop his shoulder, depositing his rider on the ground in a flash.

His trot and canter were little better than his walk but his jumping was almost flawless and what he also possessed was courage, stamina, sound limbs and a relentless (if one-paced) gallop. Above all, he possessed that intangible quality, Heart, and it made him a favourite with the South East point-to-point crowds and further a-field for a decade.

To begin with, and comparing him with his full brother Master Jock, he was a little disappointing, as he couldn't win a maiden race. In fact, he never won a maiden for half way through his second season in 1968, when he was six years old, it was decided to try him with the lighter weight in a ladies race. It was my third season with the ageing Tarkaotter, on whom I had recently broken my duck.

Rough Scot began the way he was to continue in ladies races: a second, followed by two wins. He was the easiest possible horse to ride; you could put him anywhere in a race, front, middle or back, and he never pulled. He met virtually every fence plumb right and was as agile as a cat– maybe that comparatively short stride helped him, for mistakes were few and far between. He became the nearest thing to a racing certainty to place in ladies races – yet early on he came perilously close to never running again.

It was when brought into a barn with three others after his summer holiday at grass when one of them, who knows which, kicked him in the shoulder.

We came in next morning to find Rough Scot standing there, one leg hanging. It looked curtains. He couldn't walk – but it wasn't broken. The nerves were severed and would never repair, resulting in a permanent indentation from muscle wastage the size of a man's palm. Instead, slowly, slowly, Rough Scot learnt to bring other muscles into play under the guidance of Ronnie Longford, an equine chiropractor from Warwickshire who was ahead of his time. Rough Scot walked for I don't remember how many weeks. He was certainly expected to miss the coming season, yet through a mixture of patience, perseverance and his own indomitable spirit he made it back to the track for two races, winning the second one.

How to pick out just a few of his races? The memorable trip up to Moulton in East Anglia where both he and Master Jock won, a 125-1 double; his three consecutive wins at the West Kent.

For the last of these he was ridden by my sister as I had a broken collar bone. When I returned to the saddle at Charing Rough Scot not only put his best foot forward yet again, but also his smoothest so that my injury never got niggled. During the painful early days, I had vowed never to dismiss it as 'only a collar bone'. Charing, in contrast to Heathfield, was a long, narrow oval, gently climbing uphill up the long straight by the cars, a narrow gallop across the top where the wind could hurl itself into your face and where somehow the sound of galloping hooves was magnified, then swung left-handed downhill parallel with the A20 and past The Swan public house, before straightening out for the last half mile, round the final bend and with one fence in the home straight before the winning post. It was a course to give a great racing thrill and was always well prepared.

One time, at Heathfield Rough Scot was beaten a head by Gillian Kelleway, wife of jockey and flat trainer Paul and mother of flat trainer Gaye; she was riding Brilliant Knight; two weeks later, over the same course, the result was reversed by the same short margin.

Rough Scot is followed by Brilliant Knight (Gillian Kelleway) at Heathfield. The combinations met twice at the Sussex track, victory going to each, with only a head dividing them on both occasions. Behind (partly obscured) is Ann Underwood on course specialist Bebe Fare.

It was also the course where, one time, Rough Scot and I were beaten at 5-1 on in a three-runner race; Rough Scot had won at Charing on the

Saturday and was expected to do so again in front of the Easter Monday crowds, but he was beaten by the course specialist, Bebe Fare whose price of 3-1 was so attractive that the bookmakers were cleaned out. Rough Scot gave a couple of coughs the next day.

In 1970 at eight years old Rough Scot was at his zenith: he won six races, was second twice including to the country's leading combination of Tenor and Sue Aston at the Melton Hunt Club fixture, but in one other I was knocked out of the saddle by a falling horse and rider; Rough Scot, bless him, kept his feet, that's how clever he was.

His busiest season came at nine years old with ten runs: three wins, four seconds, two thirds and ended with a fifth when tried on a NH track over a distance too short for him.

His exploits earned him the award as Leading Horse in the South East point-to-point area, Margaret as leading owner, and was the major part of giving me the area ladies jockey award – presentations that were greeted with much champagne and celebrations.

End-of-season Laurent Perrier awards, r to l Margaret Holland (leading owner), Robert Hacking (leading gentleman rider), author (leading lady rider), and sponsor representative. Behind, centre, Stan Luckhurst, huntsman West Kent and, r, Jack Champion, huntsman Old Surrey and Burstow.

The champagne was presented by and shared with the dishy Vicomte from Laurent Perrier.

More celebrations at The Mast Head, l-r the author, Bob Hacking, Ann Blaker, Ann Underwood, Jill Ditton, Guy Peate, Julie Hacking.

When Patsy and I started racing there was only one race per meeting open to us, the Ladies so, as we have seen, we tried to run on alternate weeks. A cancelled meeting could make this difficult and so it was that we both lined up for the West Street ladies race at Aldington, East Kent on March 27th 1971. The other nine runners might just as well have stayed at home, as on the second circuit the two stable companions drew further and further ahead. Patsy's mount, Aultroy, a speedier flat race winner, was never unplaced that season, winning one. Patsy, also a good rider on the flat, rode like the very devil that day. She was going so fast into one fence about two or three from home that I remember thinking, 'Crikey, we can't get away with this speed.' But I didn't want to be 'half-lengthed' and risk coming down that way, so there was nothing for it but to go with her. Half-lengthed means a horse being that distance behind a rival going into a fence, but taking off when it does, and not making it safely to the other side.

Future chasing stars and likewise next-door stable companions Kauto Star and Denman would have had nothing on Rough Scot and Aultroy that day!

Mother, watching the two of us gallop towards the last neck and neck, apparently cried, 'my daughters, my daughters' and a kindly bystander, thinking she was referring to toddlers, offered to take her to the 'lost' tent in case we'd been taken there.

Her nerves weren't helped at the last fence. I don't know what happened there, but Rough Scot made one of his rare mistakes; I was all but unseated, and I swear it was the thought of my sister hot on my heels that helped me defy gravity. I managed to get a black eye from my whip, though.

Last fence at Aldington, Mary Crouch leads on Hasty Exit but Rough Scot just got up. Con Afecto, Jean Oyler, behind, obscured, 1970.

AGAIN in the Ladies' Race and an exciting finish as two sisters fight a duel near the finishing post. As they came over the last fence, Anne Holland, leading on Rough Scot, was nearly unseated, but recovered and went on to beat her sister Patsy, who was close on her heels, riding Aultroy. Both horses are owned by the girls' mother, Mrs. Rex Holland, of Frant.

Almost unshipped at the last, but my sister is breathing on my heels. A memorable race between sisters and stable companions, Rough Scot and Aultroy, at Aldington

Rex and Margaret Holland with daughters Anne and Patsy, after their epic duel at Aldington, March, 1971.

Riding Tenor for Mr Kenneth Dale, 1973. Photo Jim Meads

Rough Scot was side-lined again in 1974 with a problem behind, and he was taken to Newmarket to be the first public horse ever to have his back x-rayed. All it showed were the spavins he had been born with! And yet again, he made it to the track for four runs, winning first time out.

The next year he was twelve years old and his heyday was past, but he ran seven times, winning one and placing in four. And now he was in training again for the 1975 season.

Cheeky and Charlie

Most of the lambs were born at the far end of the field, down near the dell, making it exhausting work carrying them up to the barn. A pair of frail twins, still wet, wriggled in my arms, covering me in mess – soon washed clean by the rain – and we put them in the 'intensive care' unit.

It froze hard again that night, but with innate optimism and for the sake of sanity, we convinced ourselves things could only improve.

They did not.

With sploshes and squelches after the frost thawed, my gum-booted feet set forth into the lambing field and I was as soaked as if it was still raining; later in the day it poured again.

The first ewe I tried to bring in was so bolshie she couldn't care less about her lamb. Next there was a fretful one, indignant at my intrusion. She snorted through twitching nostrils like an enraged bull. All created problems as we slipped and shivered up that slope.

Many had individual features, like old Big Teat; others had a curly fringe giving a boyish look. Then there were the escape experts, instantly recognisable by their loss of wool, left behind on various fences they had squeezed through. Some were gentle while others, probably those lambing for the first time, were wild and furious. These were the ones that sent us haring after them, with our exchanges becoming bluer each time.

The Houdini experts delighted in finding new ways of getting out of, around, under, and sometimes even over 'sheep-proof' fencing.

We struggled to bring in a weak ewe, one pushing, one pulling, trying to keep the poor creature on her tottering feat in the quagmire.

'Has she got pneumonia?'

'Probably calcium deficiency.'

'If only we could make her understand we're trying to help.'

Eventually we dragged her in and made up another pen. The previous day's weak lamb had survived the night but looked pretty sickly. I brought in a tiny one whose mother had no milk and T found another abandoned, tucked under the hedge curled in a tight ball shivering on the cold, wet mud patch, its mother nowhere to be seen.

'We'll have to make up some milk powder,' T looked down at the sorry lot.

It was an excuse for a break ourselves and afterwards we brought down two plastic bottles filled with warm lamb powder milk, topped with red teats. It was sleeting again and only the thought of how much worse it was for the feeble lambs kept me going.

T tried to make the previous day's lamb suck from its mother while I set about teaching the two new ones how to take the bottles. The tiny one was short bodied and had a pinky brown face. Its coat was still covered in dried yellow because its mother had never even cleaned it. I put the teat to its tightly shut lips, prised them open and popped it in. Milk oozed out from the side of its mouth in frothy bubbles, and the milk seemed to be dripping anywhere except down the little chap's throat. He dropped his head into my lap. Carefully picking it up again, almost afraid that it would drop off such a tiny body, I tried again, lifting up his chin towards the bottle, my fingers prising open his mouth, his chin cupped in the palm of my hand, the bottle upturned in my other hand, this time pushing it in gentle in and out movements.

Bottle feeding the orphan lambs

A drop of milk must have found its way down his throat for suddenly he got the taste for it and he gave a little suck, drawing in his cheeks making two big dimples, his eyes dimly making out the shape of the friendly bottle. He sucked again and, flushed with his own achievement, sucked in more and more until half the bottle was gone. Carefully I laid him down in the straw. He promptly struggled to his feet with new-found energy and gave me a little nudge.

'No, that's enough.'

He persisted and succeeded in getting hold of the teat from the bottle laid on the ground. I pulled him off and dropped him unceremoniously in the corner while the next lamb had his turn, but the first one was quickly back, getting hold of my thumb cheekily and tugging at it hopefully. He glanced upwards at me as if expecting a scolding.

'Cheeky,' I chided him gently, and in return for this christening he tweaked my little finger, his moist tongue curling round it optimistically.

Charlie

The second lamb was taller than Cheeky but thinner. It looked as if his coat was several sizes too big for his frame, hanging loosely over his bones with no flesh to speak of to fill it out. He looked at me from his corner unafraid, just slightly questioning, as if to say, 'Would you mind telling me what all this is about? I thought I was meant to have a mother to cuddle up to and keep me warm and fed.'

'Come on then, see if I'll do; you look a proper little charlie, poor thing.' Of course, the name stuck.

I never bothered to look underneath then, when my main concern was to get life-giving food into him, and by the time I discovered Charlie was a girl nothing was going to alter his – sorry, her – name.

Cheeky and Charlie did not seem afraid of their surroundings; the low barn was the only environment they knew and it gave them security, warmth and food. Both had lost their mother within a few hours of birth and they soon welcomed the red teats, snorting with delight when they saw me approaching, bottles at the ready. Cheeky cocked his head and let out a gleeful bleat when he saw me, screwing up his nose in anticipation, one ear pricked up pertly, the other flopped down beside his tiny head.

He soon moved quite quickly over the ground, not finding the difficulty in manoeuvring his compact frame that was poor Charlie's lot with her legs all at sea, splaying in every direction at once, causing her to look at me reproachfully as if it was all **my** fault. I put out my hand to stroke her but she jumped back, seeking the sanctuary of the straw. But Cheeky cuddled up, readily accepting a fuss and chewing a strand of my hair into the bargain.

Back outside, the numbering of the twins reached double figures, but too many of them were succumbing to the weather. An inch of rain in the last two days with temperatures well below freezing was caused by a cold front that had travelled from the Arctic, over Scandinavia, and on to us in a North Easterly wind – what an April!

Feeding the sheep was now a two-man operation out in the field. I led the way like one of those men who used to run in front of the first cars with a red warning flag, waving my hands and pushing away ewes, my legs straddled across the troughs trying to keep them clear for the flow of grain that T was pouring out behind me.

More lambs were abandoned, a 'guaranteed' potion did not help much, and a better bet was the warmth of the old Rayburn. We carried up Cheeky and another new pal, Number 9, in cardboard boxes to the kitchen. They clambered out and tottered around the linoleum floor, their cloven feet alternately slipping and pit-patting as they explored under the table, nosed around the Rayburn and examined the dogs' beds.

When the dogs came in, they found they had strange company. Nicky, with his nervous collie character, was at once suspicious of the new arrivals.

By contrast, Roddy, with his eternal trust, was overjoyed, licking the pair of lambs all over and wagging his tail, showing in his own inimitable way his love for all things living, friendly or not, large or small. Bred at Plumpton, within sight of the East Sussex racecourse, I had given him to T as a puppy shortly before we married. The best part of his long life came in the early days when T used to take him wild-fowling on the north Kent marshes.

Cheeky and Number 9 spent the night in the warm bathroom.

They seemed well enough to go back to the barn to re-join Charlie next day, along with a few more 'new boys.' It meant bottle feeding four times a day on top of the constant looking round the 18-acre lambing field, so I rang my boss on the paper and requested another week's 'holiday'.

* * *

My job was now with the *Sussex Express and County Herald* in a district office at Crowborough, having moved on from six memorable years at the *Kent and Sussex Courier*. T and I had been married for three years and had bought the farm, so I changed to part-time work, three days a week, and at the same time gradually built-up freelance work for *Horse and Hound* and other equestrian magazines. Fleet Street could have beckoned, but I deliberately chose to stay in the countryside. I also had my first book under my belt, *The Love of Horses*.

Reporting taught me the need to meet deadlines – always – as well as the reward in unearthing the stories behind the stories, meeting many diverse people, a love of research, and the essential requirement of check, check, and check again.

When I was originally indentured for three years, the equivalent of being apprenticed, some 95% of new reporters took that route into journalism, with 5% only coming from university. In time, this ratio was to be turned around completely, and today almost all newcomers enter via college or university. Many old hands will vouch for the method of learning 'on the job.'

One such was the redoubtable Frank Sellens, a local reporter through and through who embodied all that is good about provincial papers. He was calm and placid with a good eye for a local story in his beloved patch of East Sussex; he was always well-turned out in tweed jacket with leather elbow patches and a pipe never far away. In his spare time, he was organist in his local church, and I remember him inviting me to a performance of The Messiah in Crowborough.

Colleagues at the Courier, l-r Frank Sellens, the author, Sheila Gow, Faith Lee.
Photo Clive Osborne

Frank Sellens died 'in harness' at the age of 93 in March 2018, having dictated what turned out to be his last piece for the *Courier* just a few days before. He had given seventy-nine years' service to the paper.

When reporting one day a week at the local Magistrates' Court in Mark Cross, anyone who was convicted were named by their surname only; until then they were always Mr, Mrs, Miss or whoever, as were all other people featured in the paper. Personally, I dislike the way now men and women are referred to by their surname only.

It was remarkable, when reporting on a Golden Wedding, how often the couple concerned had 'never had a cross word in our lives.' They loved telling me about their grandchildren and great-grandchildren.

Inquests were a part of a reporter's life: paraquat, as mentioned before, or the three nuns who drove the wrong way down a dual carriageway. Then there was the man who had jacked up his car, purposely put his head under and then deliberately released the jack – I felt sorry for the jury who had to look at the photos which we reporters were spared; of tractors over-turning before roll-bars became a legal requirement; and of too many fatal r.t.a.'s (road traffic accidents). There was a 20-something-year-old young man whose sports car left the road on a slight bend in the early hours of the morning and ended twenty feet up in a tree; earlier he had been stopped by a policeman and allowed to go on his way.

The biggest and most important newspaper story to come my way was when living at Laundry Cottage; it was also to lead to something I regret deeply.

The Air Crash

It was August, 1973, before we had bought the farm. I was home from work and was running a bath and preparing a meal, oven on, when a fire engine whizzed by, blue lights flashing, siren screaming. Doubtless a chimney fire, two-a-penny. I peeled a few more vegetables. Another fire engine came by, followed by a couple of police cars. Maybe it's an R.T.A.; not a scene for me to go and gawp at, I could pick it up in the daybook tomorrow. Ambulances roared by and several more emergency vehicles. This was evidently no ordinary incident.

I turned off the oven and the bath, got in my car and followed. I needn't have bothered, for there round the corner, a couple of fields away from the cottage, was a light aircraft smashed nose-first into the ground. It was 6.30pm on a cool, clear August evening.

The pilot and his wife were dead. He had been a senior Boeing 707 pilot with more than 13,000 hours experience, and they had been to France on holiday with their seven-year-old son, flying their Beagle Terrier.

I pieced together the story. Locals and passing drivers had at first dismissed the antics of the light aircraft as aerobatics. Nothing unusual there as many passed overhead daily from the flying club at nearby Biggin Hill.

A housewife was at her farm cottage window when she heard the steady hum turn into a high pitch. She craned out of the window and saw a plane that was perilously low. The engine spluttered and cut out. Almost at once the plane picked up again, soaring upwards in a large circle. It became clear to her that the pilot was trying to make an emergency landing in a grass field beyond a field of growing corn. Harvest was on, and had that field already been combined then the pilot would probably have seen the wire fence that divided it from the grass.

The plane's engine cut out again and swooped towards the cottage. The housewife yelled at her children to dive under the settee. Now the plane took a straight line above the cornfield towards the stretch of grass beyond, where the newly-milked cows grazed in one corner. The plane was at 100feet, then 75feet, heading for the grass. Suddenly the engine fell silent. The little plane plummeted to the ground like a stone, ripping the barbed wire fence apart. It nosedived into the ground with a violent shudder, skidded and bounced like a cork in the ocean, sending up a flurry of earth and dust, leaving a crater. It jack-knifed, tearing off a wing as it did so. Then there was stillness. And silence.

The housewife and a farm-worker ran down a track to the scene. A passing car driver sent his wife on to find a phonebox to dial 999 while he thrashed his way through the ripened standing corn. At the scene they found the wife dead; the pilot died just after they arrived – but then they heard a whimper. Everywhere was the smell of petrol and it was dripping over the fuselage. And there, round the far side half hanging out of the plane, was the little boy. Alive.

His feet were trapped in the wreckage. The woman and farm-worker held him up into a more comfortable position. He told them, 'Daddy told me to jump.'

He spoke again through tears. 'He told me to undo the belt, then he pushed me. Daddy tried to push Mummy out, too.'

A policeman arrived on the scene. He also smelt petrol and saw it dripping out near the boy. The housewife held the boy's hand until the fire brigade arrived, and right through the ordeal, talking about anything she could think of. The leading officer crawled under the wing and spotted the offending petrol tank. The firemen sprayed foam all over the boy and his rescuers to prevent a spark igniting the petrol, and only then did they begin feverishly to cut away the wing, complete with tank.

A doctor arrived and gave the boy a pain killer.

'Daddy told me to jump clear,' he mumbled. 'He told me to open the door.'

Yet his seat belt still held him firmly by his waist.

At last, a hydraulic jack raised the metal from his feet and freed him. Only once an ambulance man had the tiny patient wrapped in a blanket and placed him into the waiting ambulance did the housewife leave him. The bodies of his parents had been taken an hour and a half earlier. It was a poignant moment as the burly man carried his precious load the few yards over the dewy grass in the gathering dusk.

As the ambulance trundled carefully up the track a group of small boys, legs dangling as they sat on the wall by the road, prevented by the police from coming closer, called out, 'Dead or alive?' Too young for the tragedy to hit home, only a sense of adventure showed on their faces.

The findings of the Department of Trade Accidents Investigation Branch, issued a year after the crash, revealed that an induction manifold pipe was excessively corroded and exhaust gas escaped into it making an un-airworthy mixture. The report said a pilot of his experience should have been able to cope with this by making a successful emergency landing, but for two factors: the stall warning light had been taken out in 1970 during the Certificate of Airworthiness test at the pilot's request; and his blood contained 140mg of alcohol per 100ml of blood, almost double the motorist's limit. This, the inspector said, was enough to impair judgment and ability. In addition, he was not wearing glasses which his medical certificate stipulated he should, and two pairs were found in his case, but this was not considered a contributory factor by the inspector. The inspector recommended that the internal condition of the induction manifold and heater muff assembly on that type of engine should be inspected at suitable intervals and if that was impracticable the component should be given a limited life. He described the accident as 'non-survivable' and attributed the boy's survival to his small size.

At the inquest on his parents the coroner commended the housewife, a motorist, a policeman and the leading fire officer for their 'bravery in supporting and comforting the boy during the rescue bid when there was a great danger of fire.'

The little boy went to live with an uncle in Uttoxeter, Staffordshire.

Apart from the news story for the *Kent and Sussex Courier,* followed a few months later by the report of the inquest and later the accident investigation findings, I also wrote an unpublished article about it and sent it to the uncle for approval. About nine years later, my phone rang one evening, and a slightly nervous young man asked me if I was the lady who had written an article called A Boy Lives. With rising excitement, I told him I was.

'Well,' he said, 'I am that boy.'

He'd found the article and my phone number somewhere or other in his uncle's house. We had a lovely conversation, and I asked him what he hoped to do in life.

'Well, would you believe,' he replied, 'I'd like to fly.'

It was a marvellous chat and I would have loved to talk to him again. But when T came home, he was for some reason furious and insisted I ring the uncle. It was against my gut feeling and I should have had the courage to refuse, but T stood over me and demanded I do so (I don't know why.) I rang the uncle to tell him of the call, and I never heard from the lad again.

I always felt I betrayed the young man, and with the advent of internet and social media I don't give up hope of finding him one day and apologising personally.

* * *

It was the first 24 hours that were so vital for the lambs. Usually, the weak ones drank quite a bit at first. Cheeky, of course, tugged readily, cocking his ear pertly, cheekily nosing round for more, pushing with his little bit of strength past the others to reach the bottle first. Charlie took on an aristocratic, lady-like air right from the start, often remaining aloofly to one side; sometimes the lanky lamb spurned food altogether and I wondered at her survival. Yet at times it seemed she was just play-acting. As it happened, she may have saved her own life.

Out in the fields more died of pneumonia or, more likely, they simply did not have the will to live. Lighting the lanterns one night in a particularly bad gale, the rain driving onto our faces, lashing down in near horizontal sheets, the matches sodden and ourselves covered from head to foot in oilskins, I thought of life-boatmen at sea, the hurricane lamps swinging wildly. The plastic bags blew furiously, the rain turned into sleet, and altogether it was like a vile mid-winter's night. It surely couldn't get worse.

When the sun came out for a little while next day everything seemed unbelievably better. The wind calmed down, fluffy white clouds were mere wisps scudding high across the sky now more blue than grey, the sun filtered through the oak's branches giving it a golden shimmer showing that the leaves would shortly unfurl. The lambs seemed much better and there really was a touch of spring in the air. It made us feel better, too, looking around at the beautiful countryside, the distant woods, the valley with its willow-lined, meandering flooded stream winding through. Our neighbour's bullocks grazed contentedly on the rough, heath-like hill beyond the hop-garden, and primroses and triumphant daffodils trumpeted the coming of spring from the bracken bank below the beech toll – and out in the Black Barn field our older lambs were actually **playing**! It put renewed vigour into us and we set about our tasks in happier vein. Even the suck lambs in the Intensive Care Unit all drank well.

They were joined by Mischief, the sweetest lamb who was always up to mischief in her exploits, searching for milk, exploring the pen and hopping over my feet as I sat on the hay bale bottle feeding. When she drank, she pursed her lips and looked up at me with angelic eyes that twinkled like the dew. All that one associated with spring and lambs was portrayed in her. She had been abandoned but took to me readily as her mother.

Only Charlie never lost hope of finding her real mother and was for ever jumping over the hay bales or wriggling through the hurdle bars to go and investigate every prospective new mum that came in next door. Even after she was weaned weeks later, Charlie still cried for a mother and never really took to her human substitute, merely acknowledging the provider of food. She spurned a cuddle afterwards, pinning back her ears in disgust, tucking her head round over her shoulders and looking at me disdainfully.

The break in the weather proved a one-day wonder. Next morning, we awoke to another cold, grey morning. Driving a couple of ewes up to the gate, carrying their lambs in each hand, I saw a ewe with a large lamb's head in full view protruding from her rear end; but a moment's observation showed that the birth was not progressing. Worse, the lamb's tongue was swollen, grey and dry. Lambs are born front feet first, their heads tucked in just a couple of inches behind, the whole protected in its membrane sack. Putting down the lambs I was carrying, I approached the ewe quietly but she ran off, lamb's head swaying uncomfortably between her buttocks, tongue now stiff. It looked dead, but she paused and there was a slight flicker from the lamb's head. I stole up again and tried to catch her but it was no good and by then I was convinced the lamb was dead.

T answered my call and, armed with a crook, he was able to catch the ewe. He told me to hold her head down, then, putting his hands around the lamb's head, he pulled firmly out and round, following the natural curve of birth. The long back legs gave a feeble flip as the lamb touched the ground.

'It's alive!' I exclaimed, amazed.

At once T was at its mouth, opened it and blew. He blew again and the lamb gasped, gulping in life-giving air. It shook its head, spluttering, stretched its long legs and twitched its nose. It was well and truly alive and the mother turned to lick it.

'That's a stormer,' T said. 'No wonder she had difficulty lambing such a big one.'

In the orphans' pen, Number 9 lay with his feet tucked under him, his head bobbing gently up and down. I gave him a tonic and rubbed his chest and he sucked a little before settling in the warmest corner. Cheeky cocked his head and sucked my fingers impatiently waiting for the bottle, Charlie nibbled my scarf and Mischief clambered through the hurdle bars, having been exploring. Early next morning T was walking out of the shed as I arrived with the milk with the news that Number 9 had died.

Cheeky, Charlie, Mischief and the others sucked hungrily, but there was a helping left. I shared most of it between them, and threw away the last drop, Number 9's brief fight over.

Mischief certainly had more fight in her than most. She was a rare exception and overcame troubles time and again that stronger looking lambs succumbed to. She looked up trustingly, dropping to her knees when she drank to give herself more leverage on the slanted bottle. Her upturned eyes never left mine, and frothy bubbles appeared at the corners of her mouth. The barn was quite warm, none of the old, mellow tiles leaked and the rafters were low so there was not a lot of wasted cold space. Its cobwebs had been there for years and gave it a musty smell. Hayracks lined each side of the door of the enclosed end of the barn where the lambs and sick ewes had their pens. We kept our bottles of medicine, rubber rings, iodine and equipment out of reach on top of a beam from which the crook hung. Short-stay healthy ewes and lambs were brought into the open-sided part of the barn for observation before being turned out into Black Barn or Walnut Tree fields.

We numbered the lambs and ewes there, placing the marking iron daubed in paint firmly on each side, so that if one got separated, we knew to which ewe it belonged.

'What number is next?'

'Twenty-nine.'

T picked up the appropriate irons and placed them side by side on the first twin.

'Oh, dear,' he looked at it and laughed. 'I've put the nine on first, this one says 92!' So out they went into the field, numbers 92 alongside 28 and 30. Later we moved all from that field up to the paddock by the cottage, leaving the Black Barn field for the next bunch.

Among the orphans, Cheeky, Charlie and Mischief started scouring, especially Charlie, bright yellow liquid pouring out and clinging to her tail making it look like a bit of chewed string, rather than a fluffy 'lamb's tail.'

Charlie seemed quite unconcerned and scampered off over the straw and through the hurdle to investigate a prospective new mum, eager for a comforting suck and bit of maternal warmth, only to be head-butted bodily into the hurdle bars. Charlie barely paused to shake herself before trying again. Once more the ewe rebuffed her. Charlie picked herself up and stood, hesitating a second, as if to compose herself before her next onslaught, then she threw back her head, pinned her ears flat, and cast me a sideways glance as if to ask, 'Shall I try again?'

The ewe had lain down and for a second her back was turned so Charlie waltzed up behind her, and got to within two inches of the tempting teat protruding from a full udder. She knelt down and thrust her head forward, mouth open ready to clasp the teat, but at the first touch the ewe sprang to her feet and Charlie was knocked flying once more. She stamped her small foot in frustration at being so near and yet so far.

'Come on, young lady,' I said, catching hold of her hind leg. 'You'll just have to make do with me.'

Cheeky worried me more because he did not seem quite himself. Feeding them last thing that evening his eyes did not shine in the glow of the torch and his suck was rather feeble instead of his usual robust tug. His normally cocked ear lay flopped over, giving me grave misgivings as I bent over and tucked some hay around him. Charlie snuggled down beside him, while Mischief tried to get some more milk, craning up towards the empty bottle lying on the hay bale, her front legs nearly reaching the top. One of the 'no-hopers' had died and another looked sickly.

Cheeky drank a little in the morning, a tonic added to his milk, but he had lost much of his irresistible, cheeky air. The weak lamb had died during the night but I just did not feel like starting the day by chucking out dead lambs, so turned away.

We spent 15 minutes longer than usual over breakfast and paid the penalty. Another strapping big lamb, 'a real stormer' as T would say, had been born but its mother failed to lick it and a thin film of mucus covered its face, smothering its nose and mouth. T wiped it clean, blew down its mouth and massaged its heart, but it was too late.

'Ten minutes earlier and we could have saved it,' he muttered. 'We should never leave the lambing field, there should be someone walking round it every minute.'

XII

The Last Straw

And still we attempted to go racing. Mostly throughout my career I rode our own family horses, but a number of spare rides for outside stables came my way, too. Only twice did I ride for betting stables. The first time was in the hills of West Wales, so remote that Welsh was the first language. I had been due to ride a horse called Hill House who will be a familiar name to older NH racegoers. He had infamously won the Schweppes (now Tote) Trophy handicap hurdle at Newbury in 1967 for Ryan Price who was an inspired, brilliant trainer who also liked to lay out a horse for a big bet. After Hill House won, a dope test showed that he had a quantity of cortisol, 'a non-normal nutrient', in his blood. Ryan Price was banned, but one of his owners, Lady Weir, contacted a leading cancer scientist who specialised in cortisol. After extensive tests over a number of months it was proved beyond doubt that Hill House was so excitable that he produced his own cortisol. Ryan Price had his licence reinstated and Lady Weir, as if by divine reward, won the 1969 Cheltenham Gold Cup with What A Myth. What an ignominious demise it would have been for the WW11 commando had Ryan Price not been reinstated.

However, Hill House was inclined to be a real rogue, and ended up refusing to race at all.

Now he was in remote Wales and perhaps hunting would sweeten him up. I sat on him in a canter – he had a fine sloping shoulder and big presence – but for some reason he couldn't run in the point-to-point. (When he did eventually run, it was back to dogging it and refusing to race, although he also placed in a few point-to-points in the Cotswolds.) I rode another horse and while nice enough he was not in the same class as Hill House, but the owner nevertheless had a big bet on him – and coming third wasn't good enough.

The second occasion was close to home and for a very well-known owner. Again, it was made plain to me that a large bet was riding on the outcome. It was still in the days of one ladies race only per meeting, and the mare was odds-on favourite. The course was at Mollington, near Banbury, a nice galloping track with a fair uphill and a long, downhill sweep, a lovely sort of course to ride. But the mare didn't run a yard, and it wasn't because she was in season; she gurgled loudly and had plainly swallowed her tongue (these days a tongue strap is used on a horse with this propensity and, like blinkers or recent wind operations, has to be declared in advance of the race so that the betting public knows about it.) Anyway, with the mare unable to breath properly, I had no alternative but to pull her up. The owner never asked for any explanation; he never said a word, but pointedly, when I rode back in, he walked away.

By contrast, one of the nicest owners I ever rode for apart from my mother (who never complained whenever I fell off) was Jean Oyler in Essex. It was 1970 and at the end of the previous season Jean took an horrific fall at the Melton meeting and broke her neck; although she wasn't paralysed it well and truly 'crocked' her. At the time she had two very good mares called Con Afecto and Dynusa, both home-bred and she asked me to ride them the following season. What an opportunity! Girls could still only ride in ladies races and the championship was usually won by a lady with two good horses at her disposal; with a pair like these plus our own, I must stand a realistic chance, given luck, of attaining the title!

I visited their farm in Southminster – John Oyler was a large, kind farmer and a great support for Jean – and had a day's hunting on one of them with the Essex Farmers.

Before long it was off to Cottenham, not far from Cambridge, for my first race on Dynusa, a mare renowned for jumping sharply right-handed. It was a big early season field and we eventually finished sixth, after which the redoubtable Jean declared herself fit enough to take over the reins again (no medical card, rider's licences or doctor's examinations in those days). She promptly won her next four races plus one more later in the season.

John Oyler eventually died and until 2020 Jean and I always corresponded at some length every Christmas, but she, too, died in spring of that year. She had spawned a dynasty of grandchildren as well as many descendants of Dynusa.

An owner who had every right to walk away from me but who acted like a gentleman was Joe Turner, with at the time the all-conquering stable nationally. His son, David, and daughter, Josie, were usually champion male and female point-to-point riders, and Joe was invariably leading owner.

One year, when Josie was not riding due to pregnancy, I was offered the ride on Portroy at the Torrington Farmers in Devon, the season's last point-to-point with an end-of-term atmosphere. It was a long, long drive from Ampton in Suffolk for the Turners' two horses, both of which were odds-on for their respective men's and ladies' open races. Portroy was a nice but very small chestnut, and he was going well when we went through a field of plough (long since gone) and at the next fence he pecked and off I went over his head. If only my team-chasing days had been in parallel with racing instead of after, because it was only then that I truly learnt to slip the reins and stay on board in such circumstances. As an 'amateur amateur,' that is, my day job had nothing to do with horses, it would also have helped me enormously had there been the jockey coaches of today.

David's horse was beaten a questionable short-head (no photo finish in point-to-points) and I had been unseated, but Joe Turner uttered not a word of reproach.

Another spare ride was also a small chestnut, Comci Comca, owned by Mr D.R. Haigh from Essex. He was dynamite! And very unlucky not to win.

My policy was always to ride out on a horse at its home, often schooling as well, and for this horse we travelled up to the Links on Newmarket Heath. He pinged a couple of fences and then set off at a gallop around the heath, not once, but twice, and while I tried in vain to regain control, T did his best to distract the owners by talking to them about how well he looked. Eventually I managed to pull him up – and went on to have some super rides, finishing fourth, third, and second, the latter on the sharp track at Detling, Kent. That suited his front-running tactics, and it was only after the last fence that he was caught. He didn't stay a full three miles but he was exhilarating to ride over fences; he would land 'running' while those that had jumped beside him were still in the air.

Comci Comca was small, athletic and so quick over his fences that he would 'land galloping' as illustrated here. Josie Bothway (nee Turner) on the right, Ann Blaker, left, at Higham, Essex.

The owners, understandably, decided to try different tactics and engaged a top lady rider. She 'anchored' the little horse in midfield, nearly 'pulling his back teeth out' in the process. He hated it and didn't run a yard. If it had worked, he would doubtless have conserved enough stamina to win races, but that was not his style.

A spare ride who I would rate one of the worst pointers I ever sat on but with owners as nice as you could find also gave my stepson Tim his first ride in a point-to-point, and T rode her as well. She once scraped home for a third place and the owner gave me the only 'present' I ever received racing – a silk headscarf. Tim also rode Log down on Exmoor at the end of one season when the South-Eastern circuit had finished.

The rain continued to pour in 1975 and yet more meetings were lost. Things weren't too good in the lambing fields, either.

* * *

Cheeky would not touch his milk at lunch and Charlie spurned it, too, although she may have managed to pinch some from an unsuspecting ewe next door. Outside it was raining for the eleventh day in the last 14. Yet another point-to-point was cancelled. Cheeky started a disconcerting habit of leaving Charlie and crawling up to two dead lambs in the corner, adopting the 'toy dog on the back shelf of a car' stance. Gradually his bobbing head gave less of a bob, dropping lower and lower, finally resting his face on the back of the dead lamb in front of him. He stayed like that most of the next day until he died. He had deserted his old pal Charlie and seemed determined to join the dead ones.

It was the last straw.

Tears streamed down my face half way through supper and a painful lump lodged in my throat.

'Try not to think about it,' T comforted. 'Perhaps you shouldn't really name them.' Then, trying to brighten me, 'I saw Charlie jump right over the haybale today.'

The gesture broke my final, thin thread of resistance. Through choking sobs, and heaving chest I spluttered, 'I only n-named the ones I, I thought would live... Oh, no, they're all dying. Charlie will be the, the, the... next... one.'

T persuaded me to phone a widow friend on Romney Marsh who had a lifetime's experience with orphan lambs. She was a kindly, practical person but what she said was horrifying.

'You must not feed the milk too warm or it will scald the young lambs' tummies, and you mustn't feed them too much or they will scour.'

I told her they all seemed to drink well when they first came in, nearly half a tonic bottle, giving me initial encouragement, and then they went downhill fast.

'They shouldn't have any more than an inch at a time the first day,' she said, 'and two inches on the second.'

From then on milk rations were both reduced and cooler but it did not really make any noticeable difference. Mischief scoured badly and every time Charlie had a 'no milk for me just now, thank you very much,' mood, I was convinced she was going to die. My confidence had evaporated and hope seemed forlorn.

A couple of days later, an important interview with an author could be put off no longer, the deadline for the story clashing with lambing. One appointment had already been missed, and the new one was due for 7pm in a Tunbridge Wells hotel. At a quarter to seven I ran in from the fields, soaked and frozen as usual, and ran a hot bath. The blessed relief it gave me made getting out a bare ten seconds later hard, but I raced into town where the author sat waiting, her manicured hands clasped stiffly in her lap below a perfectly made-up face. She gave me a frozen smile of welcome. But she wanted the publicity and she softened at my apology for being late, trying to explain the situation that she patently did not comprehend.

'When I lived in New Zealand, we had 2,000 sheep on the ranch but I don't particularly remember the lambing being difficult,' she said pointedly.

With no reply forthcoming, she relented slightly. 'Perhaps I didn't know all that was going on outside from within the house.'

Two years later, in 1977, she won the award for Romantic Novel of the Year.

* * *

It was a little warmer next day. Checking through a bunch of older lambs we found some pitifully thin ones, especially the pair of number 13s. Then I saw the number 17s. It didn't seem possible for lambs to be so thin and yet survive. One in particular stood with her back hunched up in an arc, every rib showing, and her gaunt, hairless head had large, wide-apart eyes staring out of great sunken hollows. She had big, scaly ears without a trace of wool, a long jaw and square mouth. In all she was quite the ugliest, skinniest lamb imaginable.

So Skinny Lizzy came into my care but I didn't hold out much hope for her. Number 13 was allowed to return but he would surely need luck to survive.

Lizzy's body moved strangely inside her loose skin, but she responded to nursing, learnt to suck from a bottle and swallowed a tonic. Nearby, Mischief sucked like mad, pursing her lips into an angelic 'O' reminding me of Christmas card pictures of young choristers singing. Charlie had grown a little but she was still scouring badly.

A surprise greeted me next morning, for there was the mother of Skinny Lizzy and the number 17 brother waiting at the gate of the Black Barn field calling for Lizzy. Obviously, it had been a mistake to bring in Skinny Lizzy for she must have been getting milk from her mother after all. I peeped over the orphans' door and Lizzy was standing by it away from the others who were still huddled together after their night's sleep. Lizzy was bleating back to her mum, her staring eyes and bald face looking up hopefully, her wide, plain ears sticking out as she listened to the familiar sound of her mother, looking utterly ridiculous.

'Come on then, you poor thing, your mum wants you after all,' and I carried her out. It was a big reunion. Mother and offspring ran towards each other, bleating, acting as if their arms were outstretched ready to embrace each other after the ordeal of almost 24 hours separation. The mother sniffed Lizzy excitedly and knickered in delighted recognition. Lizzy for her part went straight to the milk bar but suddenly the ewe jumped sideways. Surprised, Lizzy tried again.

This time she was butted away in no uncertain manner by the mother's head. I was amazed. She so obviously knew her lamb, and had waited by the gate all night for her, yet now she rejected her. I left them, thinking Lizzy would soon be totally re-accepted. On every visit during the day, there was Lizzy bobbing along in her disjointed manner accentuated by her thinness, beside her brother and mother, every bit one of the family, until the moment that mattered most, and she was rebuffed repeatedly. Her gangly hind legs appeared to shove up her spine into its hideous arc, her big ears, staring eyes and plain face making her look more like one of the ugly sisters or something out of a ghost story than anything to do with pretty spring lambs.

By evening the extraordinary situation had not resolved itself and although the mother would let Lizzy lie down with her, and would lick her, Lizzy had not had any food at all, so again she was brought in.

She never saw her mother again, and her mother never returned. Funnily enough Lizzy (who turned out to be a boy), always remembered his first week of life out at grass and that made him far more daring in venturing out to the yard from the pen than the others who had never known outdoor life. I saw the number 13s a couple of weeks later, and they had grown fat and well which made me wonder if we had been a little hasty in bringing in some of the weak ones.

During that week a new family moved into Walnut Tree Cottage which overlooked our Walnut Tree field, and the four children, aged from six to 15, were eager to help, the two girls in feeding the lambs and the older boys out in the fields.

Helping hands bottle feeding the orphan lambs

Simon, the second boy, was with me when I lambed my first ewe. During one of my walk-rounds, slipping and sliding in mud as ever, I spotted a ewe with a lamb's head showing. Swallowing hard, more afraid than excited, I called Simon over to help me catch her. Eventually we managed to corner her in the thorn alley at the bottom of the field and, pushing her to the ground, I asked Simon to hold her head still. The lamb's head was fully exposed, its tongue swollen. Taking off my ring and wrist watch, I knelt down. The lamb's head was dry, but the moment my hand slipped over its neck into the ewe, it was quite wet and amazingly warm as I cautiously explored further. The heat made my hand, cold as usual, tingle. Quickly I found a foot, but it slipped away. Tightening my grip and clenching my teeth, I pulled the foot forward, the ewe's contractions pressing her pelvis bone hard against the back of my hand, till the foot showed beside the head. Now I held the head with my other hand and pulled foot and head together, curving out and down. The lamb came forward in my grasp, the shoulders pushed through – and the rest of the body followed easily, slipping on to the soaking grass. Elated, I swept the film away from its mouth, cleared its nose and eyes and shook it off my hands as the lamb spluttered and choked, snuffling on the ground, struggling to find breath. I rubbed its chest and the lamb raised its head off the ground and gulped an almighty suck of air, its hind legs kicking, full of life! I tossed it round to its mother's head in expert fashion and at once she began to lick feverishly. The lamb was a great big female. We watched a while, assuring ourselves that the ewe was a good mother, and then we left them in peace and continued our walk round. Later in the day, I lambed another ewe in difficulties, but my first was the unforgettable one.

Next day, Mark, the elder son from the cottage, helped wring a miracle from an apparent disaster.

XIII

Twins, Triplets and Another Fall

'Bloody fox got a lamb last night!' T was upset and paced up and down the kitchen while the bacon sizzled.

'Oh, no, was it a good one?'

'One of the best; didn't finish it off, just bit the back of its neck and now it's paralysed. It could suckle a little when I held it to its mother but it's helpless by itself; don't s'pose it will survive.'

Mark, however, patiently held the crippled lamb up to its mother twice a day to reach milk. Frequently he tried putting it on its feet but the lamb fell back into a scrumpled heap each time, scraping its head up and down so hard against the ground in its efforts to get up that it rubbed one eye completely raw. The bite wound healed, but left a thick bulge and his neck was permanently bent downwards.

Young Mark persevered in his efforts each day before and after school and one morning, when he put Foxy on his feet once more, he actually stayed there for a few seconds, swaying, his bent head emphasising his swollen neck, his large pop-eyes trying to look upwards. He bleated haltingly and low, for his vocal chords had also been affected. Suddenly he tottered backwards a few steps, then fell, but it was a start.

Next day, Mark put Foxy on his feet again, and again he teetered backwards, steadied himself, then took a few shaky steps forward! He soon collapsed, yet within a few days, although awkward and still like a wooden toy, the lamb was moving around well enough to be able to go out with its mother for a few hours. He fell over several times and lay there scrabbling the ground with his feet until one of us righted him, but the day we saw him try a jump and a skip we knew there was a miracle. Unable to bend his neck sufficiently to feed by himself, he gradually learnt to improvise, bending to one knee and twisting his head sideways. We ensured he had enough milk by holding down the ewe once a day to help him.

Charlie, Mischief and Skinny Lizzy were joined by Snowy. What a character! For a start, he had a most unusual coat, with the front half covered in the normal tight curls, but the rest was long, straight strands of nearly white wool.

Snowy loved his tuck and he also adored human company. Invariably he was the first to grab the bottle and tugged at it strenuously as if his life depended on it. His mouth ended in an upward curl, giving him a permanent smile, and he loved playing with the girls from the cottage or snuggling up to me, tucking his head under my arm.

Charlie stood away aloofly when she saw me giving attention to a new lamb, but she deigned to have some milk before it was quite all gone. Whenever we were working on the sheep next door, Charlie still always hopped through the hurdle and watched inquisitively, ever hopeful of finding a nice full ewe's teat.

At night, when the lambs had their last feed in dusk or by hurricane lamp, Charlie appointed herself 'guard'. She was as pleased as punch when she learnt to jump up on the hay bale, practising constantly. After her last feed, while the others settled down in groups keeping each other warm, Charlie jumped up on the bale again, circled like a dog in its bed, and lay down, her head on her front feet, overlooking her flock.

We attempted without success to foster orphan lambs on to ewes that had lost their offspring but had plenty of milk. We tried spraying some pungent mixture up the selected ewe's nose, supposedly to make her lose her sense of smell, but that turned out to be another sales gimmick. We tried penning the ewe so tightly that she could not turn round and butt the lamb – but it didn't stop her kicking it.

When we first tried skinning, it was raining yet again. With jeans clinging to my knees like wet fish on a cold marble slab, a lost lamb in my arms, I squelched my way round to T, soaked too, his clothes also having given up the unequal struggle. He held a dead lamb, its mother waiting nearby in a forlorn hope that somehow it might come alive again.

T pulled out his penknife and swiftly skinned the dead lamb as if it was something he had done all his life. Popping the orphan into its new coat, hind legs through the appropriate holes, he tied it up under the belly and round the chest with binder twine. It had been a good-sized lamb that died and its skin swamped the living one, making him resemble the Archbishop of Canterbury in his huge cloak, so big that he nearly tripped over it as he tottered forward. The ewe looked surprised when she saw him but, ever hopeful, leant forward and sniffed. To her utter astonishment she discovered it was 'her' lamb. The expression of total joy that swept across her face as she recognised the smell, bleated softly and it answered 'maa-aa', was unforgettable. It was her own miracle that her dead lamb had come back to her. It was such moments that made everything worthwhile.

Spud (because his new overcoat resembled a jacket potato skin) and his adoptive mother stayed in for a couple of days until we were certain they had accepted each other, and removed the coat.

The skinning success eased the orphan lamb situation tremendously and there were very few failures. Snowy was one, almost certainly because he loved human beings and their associated milk bottles which he sucked with such fervour.

An obvious candidate was Lizzy who had spent a week in the field before coming in, and was quite adventurous. When we put him into his new coat it literally swamped his skinny frame, the front part stretching down to his ankles, and the hind legs so voluminous that he tripped at almost every step. He looked like something out of a strip cartoon. But the main thing was for the mother and 'son' to take to each other, and this they did at once. In fact, Skinny Lizzy escaped from the barn during his first night in a skin and next morning he was in the Black Barn field, as innocent as sin, patiently waiting by the gate to be reunited with his 'mother' in the barn.

Back inside the pen, Charlie was not drinking much again, so I administered a tonic. Mischief did not scamper up as usual either, and a second later I saw why – she was lame.

'Well, she's obviously been up to mischief,' I told the children who were eagerly waiting to help.

She looked up at me sweetly, a drop of saliva frothing the sides of her lips anticipating the milk. She looked quite sorry for herself as she hobbled up, but not worryingly so. She fluttered her long eyelashes appealingly in spite of her limp and I turned my attentions to Charlie who hunched her back in more concerning fashion – or was she having me on?

Next morning a pair of twins kept running up to a ewe that had died in the night, pawing her, wondering why she would not move or, more importantly, give them milk. It meant two more cases for the orphan wing, and to our surprise the lively beggars were the 92s! We had laughed when they were numbered 92 instead of 29, and of all the many we had numbered they were the very pair to return. The local hunt kennels obliged again in collecting the fallen ewe.

The 92s were nearly identical twins, the only difference being that one had pure white ears and the other had pinky brown tips. White Ears was a boy and Brown Ears a girl, and they certainly livened up matters in the barn. Mistrustful of us and full of health and vigour, having obtained natural succour for nearly three weeks, it was impossible to keep them inside the pen made up of hay bales. To catch them for milk I had to corner one at a time, make a grab and then carry it kicking and protesting back: the Terrible Twins indeed.

White Ears was the first to tame up a bit and it was while Brown Ears was still wild that I caught her one day exploring the empty milk bottles that were in a bucket while she thought my back was turned. She tip-toed up to investigate and pulled at one of the teats, but fled in terror the moment she saw me looking, like a schoolchild caught at the tuck tin when out of bounds. In fact, Brown Ears so loved her food that before long she became tamer than White Ears and as she drank more, she started leaving her brother behind in size as well. White Ears was always on the timid side and gentler than his sister who soon became the most demanding and bossy of the bunch.

As if they had not poured out their last reserves already, the heavens opened again on Friday, floods increased, and yet another point-to-point was cancelled. Saturday, which would have been race-day, dawned infuriatingly sunny but the warmth was welcome. Walking up the track from the barn for breakfast we noticed a couple of ewes out in Beechy Field; conscience got the better of us, and hungry stomachs waited while we rounded up the escapees. Just then we spotted another ewe against the far fence, stuck on her back, and ran towards her. Seconds later T delivered a tiny lamb.

'Why did she have difficulty lambing such a small one?'

'I think we're just going to find out,' and T gently put in his hand again. 'There are two more!'

A few minutes later the triplets lay down beside their mother, basking in the sunshine.

'If only this weather stays better, they must have a fair chance of survival, the ewe has plenty of milk,' T said, pulling at her teats, sending a jet of white liquid spurting into the air. It needed to be an exceptional ewe to rear three lambs and we crossed our fingers for these.

The next three days were recorded in my diary as 'beautiful', 'sunny', and 'hot and lovely'. For three whole days the birds sang as they built their nests. The graceful thrush with her speckled throat and chest was nesting somewhere in the garden, the sparrows in the garage eaves, and the starlings under our roof, the sounds of their pattering feet magnifying at dusk to resemble herds of elephants above our heads, then their chattering voices reminding us in no uncertain terms at first light that it was time to get up.

It was raw again on the fourth day but dry and for the first time in our area a midweek evening point-to-point, postponed from one of the waterlogged Saturdays was held – and in spite of 'distractions off' we were eager to go. It was at Aldington and as we travelled through to east Kent the apple orchards were in glorious bloom and lambs were playing king of the castle over a fallen bough. Rough Scot was second in the ladies race, and as it turned out, that was to be his best place that year; and T was fifth in the adjacent hunts race on Log.

The blissfully warm weather returned for a day although a tummy bug knocked out what little remained of my stuffing. The lambs compensated with their trust as I sat hunched on the hay bale feeding them. We had acquired an exceptionally thin one (known as Thin One) and we marvelled at how he kept going. Mischief's condition was worrying because she had a bad eye that had worsened, and although being treated with ointment it had developed a large blister, almost closing it up. She was still lame and, worse, her scouring had returned. Yet still she purred with her distinctive bleat, licking her lips for food, her good eye as adoring as ever. Snowy smiled at her with his seraphic grin, and his half and half coat never failed to cause amusement.

As for Charlie, she sat on the bale beside me and, evidently tiring of waiting for her turn at the bottle, decided to nibble the hay. It was the first time any of them had tried anything solid. After feeding they hopped out into the yard, the smaller ones staying close to the door watching White Ears and Brown Ears playing tag, joined by Snowy and watched from a cautious distance by Charlie, her arrogant air hiding her uncertainty. Brown Ears and Snowy spotted Roddy the Labrador tied up the other side of the fence and trotted up to him, sniffing through the wire. The moment he moved his broad, black head Brown Ears ran off in alarm but Snowy let the old dog lick his nose quite happily.

Except for Mischief and Thin One the lambs could now all jump up on the hay bale and they decided it would be fun to knock the bottles for six. They held a skittles competition to see who could knock over most, followed by tug-of-war matches with the teats. When they began their games before they had had their milk, sending it pouring into the straw so forcing me back to the cottage to mix more, a halt had to be called. So I placed a second bale on top of the first, putting things well out of reach of even the most ambitious lamb, although Charlie fancied herself as a high jumper and thrust herself manfully at it, looking up in startled surprise when she found herself reeling backwards.

* * *

Lambing was meant to be easing, so we took an abortive trip to Essex for a point-to-point ride, the local one having yet again been cancelled. This was the only time I broke my own rule about always sitting on a 'spare ride' at its owner's home first.

It was a horse from East Anglia called Arctic Blizzard, and it sounded as if he should be a safe conveyance, if not very likely to win. He was well-bred out of a winning mare and she had already bred seven winners. Arctic Blizzard had himself won one race on the flat but had yet to show any jumping form.

The first thing I noticed in the paddock was his 'loppy' ears, meaning his ears were so long that they flopped backwards and forwards; it is meant to be a sign of a genuine horse. He gave me a good feel cantering down to the start at Higham and was fine over the first couple of fences. The third was after a sharp left-handed bend, and as we approached it, I felt him try to duck out to the left. Strenuously I strove to pull him back to the right but the seven-feet high white wooden wing came between us. The horse crashed through it, splintering wood in every direction, and I was sprawled on the ground. Amazingly I was able to get up ok – but my thighs were visibly trembling. The horse had galloped through unscathed. Today, wings are equally high but made of much safer material.

It was yet another disaster in a season full of them. On the long journey back to more feeding of the lambs I pondered how I had found time to train at all; no wonder it was the least successful point-to-point season of my career.

* * *

When we returned, we found a dead ewe with a beauty of a lamb hovering round it. Armed with crook, T tried to catch it, but it had reached an age where it was strong, fast and wily, and human beings were definitely not on the list of friends. The lamb could really run and left us well behind. We cornered it several times but it darted out and we might just as well have been playing Tom Tiddler's ground for all the intention it had of being caught. At last T managed to make a grab and wrestled with it as it wriggled and fought vigorously to free itself. Finally, he carried it to the car.

The strange-smelling vehicle overwhelmed it and, subdued, it lay passively in my lap. She was female and simply dwarfed the others in the pen, making even the twins, Brown Ears and White Ears, look small by comparison. Poor lamb, she felt so out of place and bewildered by her new surroundings. We called her Porky, or sometimes Bessie Bunter though that insult was soon dropped when she turned out to be so gentle and friendly. She was obviously one of our oldest lambs but although she had known freedom for longer, she came to hand more quickly than Brown Ears and White Ears had done. Of course, she ran riot for a day or two but once she trusted me, she would nestle up for comfort and although she was fond of food, she never threw her considerable weight around or barged in demandingly like Brown Ears or Snowy, but waited patiently for her turn. The other orphan lambs immediately looked up to her and, although never bossy, she became their guide in the manner of a true-born leader. They got up to more pranks as well with an older lamb to follow, resembling a pack of prep-school boys.

Porky simply dwarfed the others in the pen

The task that faced us that night was far grimmer.

How I was to Rue that Chance Meeting

T went for a final walk round lighting the lamps while I fed the lambs. They tucked in well although Mischief was still lame. Feeling her leg gently for swelling or cut, I found none. Charlie scuttled in from visiting a ewe, presumably unsuccessfully, at the sound of the milk bottles, and Snowy jumped up, smiling, his forefeet resting on top of the hay bale, sniffing and searching for the teat, found it, and promptly knocked the bottle to the ground.

When T was still not back, I watered the sick ewes and gave them a portion of hay before going off in search.

It was dark in the 18-acre and sheep's eyes glistened at me eerily. Somewhere in the distance an owl hooted, a pair of bats swirled around and the lamp hanging from the oak shed a gleam on the tree's bulbous bowl. Nearby was the sound of steady munching as a group of ewes stood round a hayrack. Scudding clouds cleared a slice of moon momentarily, swiftly obliterated by more, pitching everything back into total darkness. As I struck out across the middle of the field, only the occasional bleat stirred the silence.

A roaring moan stopped me dead. It came again, stronger, louder, as though T was in agony. With heart hammering I ran forward wondering what on earth could have happened, following the sound towards the thorn hedge by the hop-garden.

'T.'

No reply, just an agonising moan of someone in great pain. 'Where are you?'

Another groan was followed by a crisp, 'Here.'

The blood rushed back to my face as I ran towards the sound of his voice. I had imagined him lying in a ditch with at least a broken leg, but it was a ewe in distress. How human a sheep could sound in severe pain! T was trying to lamb her in the dim light. She kept slipping down the bank as he pulled so I held her head to try and steady her.

'What's the trouble?'

'The lamb's been dead inside her a number of weeks; it's a dog-worrying ewe,' he muttered grimly, reminding me of the awful night when the village dogs had run through our flock. He had hold of a small leg. The ewe groaned. He pulled, she heaved, letting out a great bellow, doing all she could to shed her burden. The leg came clean away, stinking and rotten.

'If I don't get every bit of the lamb out now the ewe will die for sure,' he said. It was another full hour before he managed to finish the harrowing job. He injected the ewe with penicillin and tried to make her comfortable, with food and a bowl of water placed near her head. Numbed, we climbed up the hill in silence. She died three days later.

Things were different when the sun came out. The lambs smiled and we smiled, too. We brought in a crowd of orphans for one reason or another, all eager and guzzling. There were a couple of spare mums whose dead lambs we skinned, and fostered two orphans, but now there were 11 suck lambs scampering about in the pen, their spindly legs propelling their slim bodies disjointedly, making Charlie look quite strong!

T diagnosed joint-ill as Mischief's trouble and treated her accordingly. She was pretty lame and hobbled around with knock knees and bow legs. My lambs ventured out into the yard for a minute or two and sunned themselves, Snowy leading the way.

Some of the stronger ones followed his lead, and Mischief tried her hardest until, with a pitiful limp she, too, made it into the sun. Charlie, independent as ever, ran instead through the hurdles dividing the two halves of the barn and sauntered out of the open side into the yard, swaggering her little backside as if she owned the place, her tail shrivelled. Before long it would be gone.

Back came a steady drizzle next day. The new crowd of orphans dwindled, and two more were brought up in cardboard boxes to the Rayburn where they soon warmed up. One was still alive that evening, so we popped him into the warming oven with the door wide open, and left him for the night. In the morning, T said, 'I'm afraid we must have overheated our little chap, he's died.'

Later, a friend who had reared many orphans, said, 'You can't overheat them in a Rayburn, it's the best way of coaxing weaklings to survive,' so we consoled ourselves that ours had been a no-hoper after all and not cooked to death.

One tradition we were able to maintain throughout was family Sunday lunch with my parents at Frant. I used to call it my half-day off a week: it began with a glass of Amontillado sherry at 12 noon, sometimes with friends such as the Peates dropping by. Then it was roast meat and all the trimmings, fresh vegetables from the garden, followed by a pudding and custard, a crumble perhaps or Rex's favourite, treacle tart, the whole washed down, in my case, by cider. In the afternoon, replete, I would stretch out on the sofa – except for during lambing when it was straight back to the fray.

'I've brought you in another lamb,' T greeted me in the barn as Snowy fed hungrily at my bottle. 'She's only little but see what you can do with her.'

Tiddlypush had been abandoned in some mud under a hedge and thankfully accepted a good rub on her wet chest. She was short-bodied and covered in tiny, tight yellow curls which indicated that her mother had not licked her after birth. Tiddlypush settled down with the others while I taught another scruffy little fellow how to suck.

Scruffy took to the bottle timidly, a right little ragamuffin with elfin ears and eyes like two black buttons already losing their fear as he adapted to his strange new surroundings. He looked around at his mates – not really playmates yet until they were strong enough – and let out a little sigh. So, this is what it's all about, he thought: a cosy corner of hay beneath cobwebbed rafters and tiles, new friends, milk four times a day – but no mum. He soon learnt that in the prep school environment it was a case of first come first served, so he tugged as eagerly as the rest at the teat, and before long his frail body developed a pot belly. With his whiskers around his mouth accentuated by the remains of white milk, and his short, tottering, bow-legged stride, he looked like a little old gentleman. Although he sucked as vigorously as he could, he was not strong enough to get all the milk he needed, so his legs remained short, his body stunted. It did not perturb him, scratching unconcernedly behind one ear and snuggling up to the others. He tried jumping up on the hay bale like his bigger chums and when first allowed into the yard he was there with the others, blinking in the unaccustomed light, as he hopped off the step, tail a-quiver.

Mischief's lameness was definitely improved, but her bad eye was watery, and she was not keeping pace with Charlie's growth. Even Charlie looked small by comparison with others of her age out in the fields, plump, woolly, and skipping around especially on dry evenings. They congregated for races, tag, and king of the castle until one by one they obeyed their mother's voices to return.

We tried to save more weak twins, the 52s and the 56s. The mother of the 56s was instantly recognisable because she had a dark black patch covering half her face, the only ewe in the flock with any black on her. She disowned one of her twins and in the time it took to bring in the 52 twin suffering a similar fate, the other disowned lamb had vanished. 52, another girl and quite a character, joined the gang while in the ceaseless rain I attempted to lamb another ewe in difficulty.

She had lain down in the furthest corner of the field beyond the dell but dashed forward the moment I crept up, the helpless lamb's head swinging from side to side with the movement, its dry tongue lolling. In desperation I tried climbing through a thorn bush to reach her but only succeeded in getting scratched.

There was nothing for it but to trudge back up the hill, through the muddy gateway by the oak and fetch the crook from the barn; but even with the long arm of the law, unwieldly in my hand, she was elusive. She ran one way, I another. She pushed her way through the barbed wire fence, forcing her cumbersome body through and darted round the stagnant pond, acting more like a spirited yearling than a matron in labour.

At last, she was hooked. Now for the business end, pulling at the lamb's head. Nothing happened. My hand went above the lamb's head and through the narrowest of openings into the ewe, her pelvic bones crunching hard against my knuckles, and groped inside for a foot. Nothing doing.

'Blast, the legs must be backwards,' I muttered, large rain drops falling from the overhead branches down the back of my neck as I tried to think logically where the feet must be. It was burning hot inside the ewe and her contractions were bruising my hand.

'Impossible to put your hand in with a lamb's head out,' experienced sheep men told me later – but they would have bigger hands.

The rain streamed down steadily. The valley was flooded again and across the far side the bracken bank beneath the beech toll was changing its hue from the yellow daffodils to blue, and the lovely fragrance of the bluebells hung in the damp air. A magpie flew out and a jay screeched. Wiping the water away from my face, I shook my aching hand and tried again, but it was no good and time was running out, the lamb's tongue was badly swollen.

I was completely alone; tears of frustration and despair added more water to my face. There was nothing for it but to summon help, slipping, sliding, panting, aching, up the field, along the track to the cottage, and on to the phone, as T was away, (I wasn't sure where.) It was before the advent of mobile phones.

As luck would have it a neighbouring farmer had just got in and was round with his brother within five minutes. Roy was a big, strong man with twinkling eyes, weather-beaten face and white-toothed grin. At once he took hold of the lamb's head in his large palm and expertly pushed it right back inside its mother. Then he found the legs and neatly proceeded with a perfect assisted birth.

The huge lamb shook itself, snuffling; then it bleated. It was a ram lamb and the mother turned round to lick him proudly.

'Anytime,' Roy answered my thanks, and explained how to tackle a similar situation another time.

'If you are frightened of losing the head you can always tie some twine round the neck so that you could pull that if necessary.

'But you must push the head right back inside to enable you to find the feet.'

For the next bout of trouble, it was the vet that was needed.

* * *

Scruffy and 52 had rather fat tummies. Having long since lost track of time, some mental arithmetic resulted in me reducing the lambs' feeds to three a day. Only Brown Ears, who was growing bigger than White Ears daily, really protested at the ration cut. Tiddlypush was making better progress than Scruffy making him look scruffier than ever. Mischief had gone back with her various ailments and was now much smaller than Charlie. Whenever there was a drop of milk left over, probably from Thin One, Brown Ears and Snowy vied for the remnants, competing to see who could reach it first; unlike Charlie and Porky, this pair never left me all the while a hope remained, however remote, of finding left-overs. Once the last traces had vanished, they jiggled the bottles and tugged at the teats in vain hope of finding more.

The older lambs, Porky, Charlie, Snowy, and White and Brown Ears, began to eat some solid food, nibbling at the odd strand of hay and once or twice they investigated the corn put out for any ewes that were in. Soon they would have pellets of their own to supplement the milk.

One day I watched Charlie sample water for the first time. She approached a bucket boldly and dropped her head inside inquisitively. When her nose touched the ice-cold water she jumped back, shaking her head in surprise. Cautiously this time she stepped forward again, her round, dark eyes staring earnestly. At the second attempt she drank a few sips, glanced up in pleasant surprise, and took some more.

The lambs spent more time outside and it was time to move them from the barn and build a pen in the garden. Pressure in the fields was easing at last and the whole of one afternoon was spent in making up the new pen, commandeering some hay bales for walls, an old chicken shed door for a roof and straw on the floor. It looked quite cosy and more or less waterproof. Next, the wildly overgrown garden around it had to be fenced in, but the work with stakes, mallet and netting was comparatively easy with the ground so soft from incessant rain.

A day elapsed between making the pen and bringing up the lambs and during that day Thin One finally gave up. It did not surprise me, rather it was incredible that he had lasted that long.

The lambs were wary about the car when it was reversed into the yard. No sooner had I popped some in than others toppled out again, tumbling over each other in their anxiety to escape the evil-smelling creature. Even Mischief, with her gammy leg and blind eye wriggled her way out and the precautionary newspaper spread over the back seat was soon scrumpled up and useless. Finally, they were all in, the door shut, and with Porky sitting up like Roddy on the passenger seat, we set off. Brown Ears decided there was a bit of a squash on the back seat and promptly jumped on to the back ledge, giving an animated display of one of those nodding toy dogs! Little Mischief was pinned close up against the door but never complained as I drove steadily up the bumpy track to the cottage with the precious cargo. I carried them out two by two as if it was Noah's Ark, except for Porky who was too heavy, and popped them over the fence. They explored their new surroundings eagerly like a troop of Cub Scouts arriving at a summer camp, darting from place to place, sampling the green grass (a tasty new delicacy for them), searching out smooth places to lie down, and exploring the hay hut until they were hungry and bleated for milk.

A row of bottles placed in line on a hay bale outside the fence, their necks protruding through the netting into the pen, made it possible to feed them all at once, except for Porky who was too genteel to barge in and preferred to be hand fed, my arm around her ample waist. One drawback to the new method was that Brown Ears and Snowy, in their exuberance, would charge into the smaller lambs once they had gulped their own milk, knocking off the weaker ones and finishing their rations as well. Poor Mischief scoured again and was pretty poorly for about three days before picking up; she never lost her own special bleat. In fact, I knew most of their individual calls, Porky always gentle, Brown Ears ever demanding, Scruffy, who was looking more and more like an old gentleman with short legs, pot belly and beard, had his own voice and Charlie's was a fruity mmm-aaa which was instantly recognisable.

Porky grew even more quickly in her new surroundings and tasted every fresh morsel with relish. When she stood still and cocked her head, she looked like a top-heavy ballet dancer with her slender legs daintily pointing, best toe forward, and her knock-knees nearly touching each other. She jumped up on the fence to reach low-hanging leaves of the cherry tree on the far side and virtually climbed up the hedge to nibble the shooting buds. She was a dab hand when it came to cow parsley: she jumped forward towards a head crowning a stalk nibbled bare of leaves by the smaller lambs, breasting the stem and holding it in place with her chest. She then craned forward to bend the stalk downwards until the delicate white head was within reach. Having mastered this art, Porky made short work of the raspberry canes, stripping them bare, leaving just one or two of the highest buds for the birds to have the final picking.

Brown Ears also grew apace and became quite rough; Snowy was more sporting and took being beaten to a bottle by Brown Ears with good grace – he usually managed to find another one anyway and smiled permanently. When I approached with milk, he jumped up, his twinkling eyes imploring me, 'Please let me have some tuck, I'm **starving**.'

'Hold on a minute just let me fix it up,' I told him. Tiddlypush and Scruffy squabbled over a bottle and Mischief, in her eagerness to drink, bent down on her good knee to enable her to suck harder, but none could match Snowy's tug, grinning with delight. What a sight they made in line at the row of bottles, mouths firmly grasping teats, hind legs braced, bottoms wiggling and tails waggling. Brown Ears pawed the ground impatiently and knocked the others out of her way, yet when it came to the actual sucking, she was as gentle as the rest, just a bit swifter.

Three new lambs joined the gang, an exceptionally pretty pair of twins known as Twinnies and a good single with large, drooping ears who I called Floppy, all female.

At a suitable moment, trying to sound casual, I asked T, 'Can we keep the better ewe lambs for breeding? Like Porky?'

'Mm? Well, may be,' he said absently.

'And Brown Ears because she's a good big lamb, and of course Charlie, we couldn't let her go.'

'Bloody stupid name for a girl.'

Another disastrous point-to-point came and went. It was our local meeting at Broad Oak, Heathfield and it was a course I loved riding round. Lucky it may have been for me at times, but not that day. T's horse was balked and mine, dear old Rough Scot, now aged thirteen, took the one and only fall of his long and honourable career, at the open ditch at the furthest point away from spectators. He lay on the ground for ten minutes and my poor mother feared the worst. Then he got up, having been winded but otherwise, thankfully, uninjured.

I also managed to fall off him twice that year (how in heaven I don't know) and it was the only season, bar as a five-year-old, that he did not win. On reflection, and when considering the disastrous lambing we were going through, it should not have been a surprise.

After the fall, it was back to the lambing fray, bruised and battered, to find the orphans with fat tummies, pushing out their hind legs so they resembled wheelbarrows, but a woman buying milk powder alongside me at the agricultural merchants', was reassuring.

'I always give mine as much ad lib milk as they like,' she said. 'They get fat tummies and scour but they get over it.'

How I was to rue that chance meeting!

A few mornings later I went out to feed the lambs, the sun rising above the wood, dew on the ground and birds busily chattering as they flitted around the hedgerow, when I sensed a lamb was missing. Boisterous and hungry, they did not give me a chance to walk round into the hut until the bottles had been dished out, but the feeling that one was missing nagged. There was Porky all right, I fed her myself. Up at the bar, jostling for places, were Scruffy and Tiddlypush. There went Brown Ears knocking Scruffy off his teat and cannoning into Mischief kneeling at the far end. I was livid with myself for not identifying the missing lamb – it was probably unwell with scour inside the hut or grazing the far side without having yet heard the bottles. There was White Ears, running along behind the row of bottoms, politely looking for a gap, unlike his tomboy sister who simply barged her way in; Floppy and Twinnies were there, and there was dear old Charlie.

Just then Tim, home from college for a few days, called me urgently.

'Anne, there's a dead lamb under the cherry tree.'

With heart in mouth I ran, then stopped dead in my tracks.

'Snowy!' He had fallen over in the furthest corner, face down, front legs drawn back under him, his hind legs stretched wide apart as they had tried in vain to cope with his huge, swollen, distended stomach. He was desperately bloated. And quite dead.

Scarcely able to believe my eyes, I forced myself to take it in. Snowy, the poppet who so loved his food, must have had too much last night. So much for being advised not to worry about pot bellies. Snowy had made me laugh whenever he found extra milk and tucked into it gleefully. Snowy, with his permanent smile, his grin, his great character, wide, pinky ears and unusual snow-white coat, half in tight curls, half in long flowing strands, had above all been Fun.

Pills, Potions and Paraphernalia

With Snowy gone, Brown Ears had no serious contender for her race to the milk. I missed Snowy more than I would like to admit, but the dogs doubtless enjoyed the freshly-boiled meat that they ate for a few days afterwards. Porky and Brown Ears were growing so well, nibbling grass and some feed pellets, that it was time to cut out one meal and return to work.

One of the first stories to follow-up, along with the normal run of parish councils and jumble sales, court cases and coffee mornings, was a public meeting to discuss the amenity opportunities proposed for the 770-acre Bewl Bridge Reservoir being constructed and the valley flooded between Lamberhurst and Ticehurst. Luckily, it was an evening meeting so, as with the numerous parish councils, I could take time off in the morning to ride, feed the lambs, check round the flock and, occasionally, tend to the cottage.

Bewl Bridge was a bold initiative that involved flooding eleven houses and farm buildings and a number of country lanes. The heavy Sussex clay, a bane of my life when trying to clean off horses or jackets, was ideal, and the location near enough to supply water to the Medway towns. One house was spared. The 14th century Dunsters Mill House was removed beam by beam and brick by brick nearly half a mile up the hill, safe from flooding and, when complete, affording a beautiful view of the natural-looking reservoir, with a number of arms making an overall attractive piece of water. Apart from providing domestic water, it also became a haven for birds and wildlife, water sports, fishing, and for walking or cycling round its 12 ½-mile circumference. And these days, 50 years later, it is also used as a wedding venue.

Porky looked hurt and upset when breakfast was omitted.

'What a way to treat a girl,' she looked reproachful.

Bossy old Brown Ears was far more forthright.

'What do you think you're doing?' she demanded, boring her head into me like a prize fighter determined to win. She was livid and at lunchtime she twice jumped out of the pen, tucking up her front feet to clear the wire, and marched straight though the open door into the cottage as if she owned the place. I dropped her back without further ado but that did not stop her ranting and raving, impatient for her drink.

The lambs all came running up to the fence when they heard me drive in from work, so I strolled over to say hello before making up the milk. They were all safely inside the pen but Brown Ears, reading my thoughts, promptly leapt out, all four feet stretched out over the netting like a rather fat steeplechaser. A lamb was on the ground and although Mischief occasionally got knocked over, she usually quickly found her feet. Suddenly, as the lamb rolled over, I saw it was bloated. Rolling from side to side it resembled a barrel, and this time it was 52 who was well and truly blown.

Brown Ears leapt out, all four feet stretched over the netting like a rather fat steeplechaser

Panic stricken, I picked her up and carried her out of the pen wondering what on earth to do. Things were getting ominously like 'ten green bottles, and then there were nine.' Who was going to be the next one? I bundled her into the back seat of the car with Brown Ears jumping in for the ride and flew down Whitegates Lane, even narrower than ours, to Ginny, a neighbouring sheep farmer and horsewoman, a no-nonsense character with a good sense of humour – and much country knowledge.

Ginny's first remedy was to pour us each a large Scotch as poor 52 rolled around the floor and Brown Ears bellowed distantly from the car.

'She'll be all right all the time she keeps moving, it's rather like a horse with colic,' Ginny said, as she searched through her kitchen strewn with papers, whippets and general paraphernalia for the necessary needle with which to puncture 52's bloated stomach, but in vain.

There was nothing for it but to call the vet. Alas, he was out but expected back imminently. Half an hour and a couple of whiskeys later (breath tests had yet to really register in the countryside), the vet had returned. Arriving at the surgery, Brown Ears jumped over into the front seat and sat by the steering wheel like a dog yapping, only she was bleating.

The vet took one look at 52, hoisted her onto the operating table usually graced by cats or dogs, deftly cut away a square inch of wool on her bloated stomach, and expertly stuck in a hypodermic needle at just the right spot. Out poured the offending gasses in a series of hisses. One could almost feel the enormous relief for her as 52's side visibly deflated like a pricked balloon, releasing all that pressure. There just remained to give her a laxative, liquid paraffin, and back at home she had a little glucose in water.

It was my turn to feel relief when next morning she looked quite normal and was eagerly awaiting her milk. If only we'd found Snowy in time.

Out on the farm, T set about vaccinating the flock. Unfortunately, they crowded too closely into the pen he'd erected and four lambs were crushed to death. One was big, another a triplet. He hung them up and later jointed them for the freezer. In the more mundane world, I had my car serviced and MoT'd. The total bill amounted to £16.38p. Back on the paper, I attended a local dog show on Sunday, a fire in one of the villages, Frant parish annual meeting, an art exhibition in Mayfield, and a meeting in Wadhurst for its proposed Festival 76. I 'picked up' stories for Frant pantomime a.g.m., an old people's home coffee morning, and I also managed to go to a Writer's Circle talk in Tunbridge Wells, and a music recital in Frant church.

What happened next was less serene, although for a while we thought perhaps spring was finally making a belated appearance.

Terrifying screams woke us during the night and as T rushed out into the darkness, I lay trembling for the fate of the lambs. It was foxes all right, but fighting each other over an infringement of their own boundary laws; even so I was glad a hurricane lamp was still lit at night near my lambs' pen.

There were some positive signs that spring was at last making a belated appearance. The foxgloves were taking over from the bluebells in the woods and the tightly curled heads of bracken were slowly unfurling into their pale green lacy patterns. The woods around were mixed with dark pines, silver birch, sweet chestnut and holly. Slowly, very slowly, the oak was changing from a browny-yellow to its own green and the mighty beech contrasted its pretty green leaves against its black bark. There were even a few shoots of gentle green grass stems sprouting through the sea of mud surrounding the feeding troughs and gateway in the 18-acre.

The fruit trees blossomed but our Golden Plum bore so little that it had evidently allocated itself an enviable year off after its dramatic effort the previous autumn. Then, I had picked and bottled plums as fast as possible but still not kept pace with the wasps.

A blackbird tried nesting on top of the lambs' hut but the frequent disturbances caused her to renew her efforts elsewhere. In the early mornings, as the weak sun filtered through the arched bedroom window, there was always a rabbit crouching, nibbling in the grass, with the thrush hopping about nearby in search of worms.

I raised the height of the fence the day after 52's episode and succeeded in containing Brown Ears, at least for a while. It was a sunny morning but by lunch time ominous black clouds gathered overhead. For once I ignored them for after such a wet spring it could hardly rain so heavily again, surely. Mischief had more scour but seemed quite happy and dear 52 was as perky as if nothing had happened, wrinkling up her snub nose in pleasure when the milk arrived. Then the heavens opened. Rain poured down in straight torrents making it so dark in the cottage that I had to turn on the lights, not the flick of a switch taken for granted by most but an operation which entailed filling the generator from the tank outside while rain, diesel and spent oil seemingly poured over me in equal proportions.

Unbelievably it rained all the next day, too. Nine lambs still came out clamouring when they heard the evening milk arriving and I was drenched within seconds, but Mischief stayed in the dry hut. I coaxed her out and put a bottle to her lips but she turned away feebly. I prised open her mouth and poured in some milk, closing my wet hand around her jaw to make sure she swallowed. She was totally disinterested yet still she looked upwards, her good eye gazing into mine appealingly, and pursed her lips a little as if to say, 'Thanks for trying to look after me.' It was the sweetest expression.

It rained all night and was still coming down in sheets in the morning. An early telephone call told us that the point-to-point scheduled for that day – normally the last of the season and associated with summer clothes and an end-of-term atmosphere – was cancelled because of water-logging – it was May 17! Pulling on my faithful jacket, I ventured out into the wet. Again, nine lambs braved the elements for their tuck and, leaving them to it, I walked round to the hut. It was remarkably dry inside, the old roof had withstood the hammering well with only a few wet patches, heightening the pungent lambs' odour. Mischief was lying in the far corner where she had crawled for her last refuge, one leg sticking out stiffly behind. She may have been crushed by some of the others as they crowded in for shelter but it would not have made any difference. She had probably been asleep when she died, her brave fight against the big, cruel world finally lost. After Charlie, she had been around the longest; she had survived against many odds making recoveries that others would not. It was ironic that the heavy rain that had caused the deaths of so many during lambing had returned and finally claimed Mischief.

It brought the memories of those arduous, toiling weeks flooding back; the appalling conditions, long, wearying hours, physical effort and aching limbs. Perhaps a buoyant market in the summer would compensate.

* * *

The orphan lambs were wet and bedraggled and their coats had grown long enough for the rain to make a parting down their backs and curling Charlie's fringe. She lost her tail that day and the others' were gone soon afterwards. Still the lambs looked to Porky as their leader, and Porky looked to me as mother. They had all totally accepted their situation in life with the exception of Charlie who never gave up hope of finding a real mother.

A postponed point-to-point was held and it really was the last of the season – and still we hoped our luck would change. No way! Instead, we had three falls between us.

I was to ride Roman Receipt in the ladies race at the West Kent at Ightham; he was nick-named Romeo because he had a white eye. Quite small but compact and well made, he was a nice horse if not a world-beater – the following season he was to come in for some good luck, but not this time.

We bought him from Eddie McNally, a small local trainer for whom I used to ride out. At one time he had a horse that was ante post favourite for the Grand National and he and his wife Deirdre, his 'right-hand man', were so excited about it, doing their best to have him just right for the day, remembering to take everything necessary up to Liverpool with them, and even wondering what to wear at the dinner should he win (he was unplaced). Subsequently Deirdre – and her dog – were killed in a car crash; she was 29 and left behind young daughters and a devastated husband. It shook me horribly.

* * *

Roman Receipt had run with a little promise in 'men's' races and we thought he would appreciate the lower weight in a ladies, so I was set to ride him at Ightham. A sizeable field of ladies faced the starter, including one of the most competitive females in the country. She was, most unusually, caught napping at the start, something that annoyed her so much that she galloped furiously towards the first, cutting across my horse at an acute angle just before the fence, completely blocking it from our view. Poor Romeo had no chance of seeing it and took one of those awful head first falls where the hind legs rise perpendicularly into the sky. It should have broken his neck but thank God didn't. It nearly broke mine, receiving a whiplash as I was flung face first into the ground. It also knocked out two teeth.

In those days it was against the Rules to bypass a fence, to do so would declare the race void. Only a disc could be placed in the fence and approaching riders had to decide which side of it to jump. As I lay on the ground, conscious but pretty 'crocked', I could hear the runners getting ever closer as they approached the second circuit. The ambulance crew tending me must have been mighty brave.

It was one of those falls where the casualty is carted straight off to hospital, by-passing the first aid tent, but amazingly I was only in for three days. It was a while before I could eat properly and my neck remained in a collar for a number of weeks so my season was over; I recuperated on Exmoor for a couple of weeks with a family friend, Robin Fane-Gladwin, who had recently been widowed and whose life, unfortunately, became a tragedy. We had good fun together when I stayed, chatting – difficult with loose front teeth and two missing either side of them, eating – even harder – visiting a point-to-point, picnicking by an Exmoor stream, meeting her friends.

The overwhelming memory of that terrible fall, though, is of the number of calls to my parents and cards to me.

* * *

When I came home my lambs had grown enormously. What's more, they had been fully weaned, for the simple reason that T ran out of milk powder! Only Scruffy remained very small, his mate Tiddlypush having grown nearly as big as Charlie. We opened a narrow gap into the adjoining field enabling the lambs to roam at will but at the same time barring the ewes in the field from getting into the pen. Only one tried. She remembered the plastic feeding bag from the winter and tried in vain to squeeze in when she saw me bringing feed to my lambs. Sometimes her lamb, a lean, thoroughbred-looking type, would slip in and join the orphans, but fled in terror when I approached. Inevitably Charlie had a go at suckling this mother when she lay near the gap, but to no avail.

When the ewes and their lambs were moved to another pasture, leaving only the orphans, they explored the far side of the field, Porky in the lead, the others following in some trepidation. As they got older and bolder so they split up more but seldom went off alone. If they did, they bleated plaintively but they had no mother to call directions and for some reason none of the orphans helped their mates in this way.

Charlie walked alone only 50 yards from the pen one day, calling. The others were all near the hut but none answered. Charlie called again, pleading, 'Where are you?' Her eyes searched intently, begging for an answer, but after one more try, she gave up and lay down, alone and forlorn. On the other hand, their 'grub's up' voices were understood by one and all, and the moment one of them saw me they shouted back the good news, and all set up a chorus as they galloped up.

When the main flock was in the field too, I had to shout, 'Come on,' at the top of my voice if the orphans were out of sight. One would lift its head, immediately the Indian call went out, and seconds later 'suck' lambs emerged from all parts, galloping full tilt, as fast as their little legs could take them. They brushed aside the 'wild' lambs in their way and, now in line abreast, headed for the pen.

Porky followed me if I walked into the field and the rest stopped whatever they were doing to follow her. One day, Nicky and Roddy joined in, romping with the lambs who ran and jumped together showing no fear. Later, White Ears lay near the garage, his chubby cheeks puffed out as if he was blowing bubble gum. He came over the moment he saw me, bleating softly. He was growing too well for his own good; perhaps since he and Scruffy were the only males left, they could be kept as mascots for a couple of highly strung racehorses, especially if the ewe lambs were saved for breeding.

Porky nearly got mixed up with the wild lambs by mistake one day when the flock was being moved from the cottage field to Upper Walnut Tree. Several of the orphans tagged on at the back but at my call they ran back, except for Porky. She thought herself very grown-up being part of the flock and by the time she found she was going to a strange place she could not extricate herself, surging forward helplessly with the tide. I managed to separate her with a few others in Beechy Field, wishing yet again that we had a sheep dog, but suddenly she was afraid and unsure of herself. She darted this way and that, reminding me of when we had first found her, her cumbersome body moving with surprising agility. At last, I caught her but could not persuade her to follow me to the cottage, nor to walk at my heel on binder twine, so I tied her to the fence and dashed back for the car.

Gratefully she nuzzled the noses of her mates when safely back in the pen so, for the time being at least, the remaining gang was intact – and a welcome addition was in store.

Salutary Lesson

What a surprise greeted us when we answered a knock on the door and found a lovely bundle of highly-bred collie in Ginny's arms. My prayers had been answered! Her name was Jill, and Nicky and Roddy got on famously with her from the start. She was nearly a year old and trained to date by following her Welsh champion father.

'Does she understand English?' we enquired anxiously, imagining the chaos if she knew only Welsh commands.

Jill was a mixture of black, white and light brown, all three merging into the white tip of her bushy tail that flowed gracefully to the ground. A white stripe ran from her forehead, between her eyes, and broadened out over her muzzle with a white ruff round her neck, and white legs. The long, fluffy coat hid a tiny workmanlike frame. She was a bundle of energy and tore into the house like a tornado every evening at bed-time. One time, she was shut in the front porch while we went out for a couple of hours. The vacuum cleaner was also housed there. When we returned, every foot of its lead had been shredded into neat two-inch strips.

Jill's sandy eyes were ever alert, her ears lying back when she was relaxed but pricking up the instant anything caught her attention. She barked furiously at the generator the first few nights so we relented and brought her in. A couple of evenings later when, instead of cranking the generator into life we were eating by candlelight, she gave herself away by howling at just the same moment so, her ruse discovered, she stayed firmly put. She loved watching the birds strutting round the garden and stalked them until they flew up indignantly in front of her face.

The orphan lambs were frustrating because she expected them to run away but of course Charlie and co trotted up to her trustingly to lick her nose in friendship.

The day after Jill's arrival T kept her on a lead until she had settled down and got to know him. We wanted to 'drench' the flock against worms, trim their feet and put them through a foot bath, so we made up a hurdle pen and rounded them up to within about ten yards, then defiant ringleaders broke away. I chased after them, quickly back into the old, familiar routine of shouting and slapping hands on thighs, while T stood still, nursing the dog.

They were nearly in when the beasts staged a mass walk-out (or rather bolt out) again.

'Quick, run!' T yelled.

That did it, of course.

'Run yourself!'

'I can't, I've got the dog…'

Luckily, Jill was a quick learner, combining natural ability with the will to please and in a short time she was saving us miles of walking, running, panting, shouting and not a little mud-slinging.

* * *

The weather at last came fine and it turned into a long, hot summer so that soon we were praying for rain. The fields that had been brown with mud in the spring were now as brown as a desert, scorched by the sun. The spring rain had obviously expended itself, as none fell at all in June, July or August. We built a kennel and the lambs played sandcastles on the pile of ballast, Charlie exploring it inquisitively first. Grass became scarce because of the drought and a new fear cropped up when my lambs found their way through the hedge into the peaceful lane, occasionally used by maniacs as a race-track, so I spent a morning cutting chestnut branches to stop the gaps. By the same afternoon, Scruffy wriggled his way out again and trotted up to where I was writing in the shade of the plum tree as pleased as punch with himself. He was still so much smaller than the others that he had squeezed through and now he turned up his elfin face, his scaley ears pointing up at their tips as he bleated in cheerful recognition. His companionship made the writing easier, a sequel to my first book; this one was *The Love of Ponies*, and like the first, it was all-colour pictures with extended captions. Both books were for a modest flat fee, meaning I would get no further royalties no matter how well they did, something I never regretted, because they got me started; I still have some children's fan letters that arrived from around the world. On completion, and having helped choose the photographs for the book, I embarked on Lambs' Tales.

The lambs were shorn before the weather got too hot, to reduce the danger of fly strike, a horrible business when blowflies lay their eggs in the sheep's fleece, usually where they are a bit mucky, then maggots are born and if they are not treated in time, they literally eat a sheep alive, swarming through her wool and into her flesh in a revolting, writhing, seething mass, smelling to high heaven.

The lambs looked so bare when they were shorn that for a day or two, they were scarcely recognisable, reminding me of Skinny Lizzy when new-born, now one of the sleek, nearly fat 'wild' lambs. In spite of the warm weather the orphans sheltered in the hut again for a day or two after shearing.

At last, we got on with the garden, and that meant clearing away the lambs' hut, which Charlie sometimes tried to jump on when feeling playful but was otherwise largely redundant. Half apologising, to camouflage his soft spot, T solemnly re-built it in the field 'in case they missed it.'

Porky got up to some tricks with a bucket left behind in the field after feeding them. The temptation was too great. She nosed up to it anticipating some extra food but instead of pulling her head back when she found the bucket empty, she tried to look up, so that the bucket completely covered her head and rested on her ample shoulders. Bemused, she started shaking it from side to side but still did not lower her head to free the bucket. She staggered around with it stuck fast and the other lambs looked on curiously at the apparition, darting out of her way as she stumbled towards them, like a game of Blind Man's Buff. Then she walked straight into the fence, wedging the bucket still further so, laughing out loud, I hurried to her rescue. She looked round perplexed for a few seconds, then headed straight for the bucket again, still associating it with food and not her latest escapade, and promptly went through the whole process again.

Porky and the bucket; the other lambs ignored her antics.

She looked at me sheepishly for a moment when freed again before her seraphic smile returned and she jumped up at the hedge for tasty leaves out of reach of the smaller lambs, as if that was what she had intended doing in the first place.

It seemed a long time since Porky was a scared orphan running for her life, disguising in her distress her gentle, friendly personality; the cuddliest lamb. As Charlie, the longest survivor, pinned back her ears and cast me a proud look from her stance by the hut I remembered Cheeky, Snowy and Mischief and wished they were here to enjoy the sun. Tiddlypush, now grown so well, and 52, the only veterinary case throughout lambing, grazed near the thrush and rabbit's favourite corner (within easy reach of freshly dug worms and lupins); Floppy and Twinnies lay beneath the spreading branches of the cherry tree contentedly chewing the cud; dear little Scruffy wandered up to me and scratched behind his ear; and White and Brown Ears, the brother and sister who had been marked 92 by mistake instead of 29, strolled over towards the wood where now the foxgloves had died, and reached up to drink from the water trough.

Before long the lambs joined the main flock in the 18-acre at the far end of the farm because, I suspected, T wanted them to mingle with the others and have me forget them, a mission he doubtless knew must fail. They raced in circles round the cottage while we tried to round them up for the move, Brown Ears indelibly stamping her footprints into the newly laid concrete of the conservatory we were building between sheep jobs. Scruffy trotted over to investigate, hiding himself behind the low wall so soon a game of hide and seek was in progress. When they tired of that they practised their hurdling prowess by jumping one after the other over the stile as if they were competing in the race of their lives.

An hour or two after moving them I stole back to the sweeping 18-acres for a peep at how they were faring. All around ewes and lambs grazed peacefully but suddenly my eye was caught by a movement in the distance. As it came closer, I saw the outlines of nine of my lambs walking slowly but determinedly over the brow of the hill and, without hesitating, on into the Black Barn field, where they had the whole ten acres to themselves.

Porky was the missing one, and she remained with the flock; she was soon re-joined by Floppy, and they were seldom far apart thereafter. White Ears, The Twinnies, 52 and Tiddlypush made their home happily enough in the Black Barn field but when we got up next morning, we were greeted by a trio of visitors on the back door step: Charlie, Scruffy and Brown Ears had come home! They had found their way from the 18-acre and Black Barn fields, through Upper Walnut Tree, along Beechy field, picked their way through the wood, skirted the pond and found a hole into the home paddock, back over the stile – and there they were, triumphantly home again.

There they stayed, too, and although I tried to confine them to the field, they discovered that the roses were too great a treat to be given up easily, and found so many different ways of getting into the garden that I could not keep up with them; they did at least help keep the lawn mown and the beds fertilised!

The roses were too great a treat to be given up

Flowers bloomed in the garden, clusters of honeysuckle climbing up the cottage filled the air with its fragrant sweet scent, and over in Walnut Tree field a tiny lamb with gangling legs, minute body and closely curled coat, born many weeks later than the rest, bleated plaintively, its voice so young and tremulous that suddenly I realised I had almost forgotten the sound of a new-born lamb now that the orphans' voices were throaty and adult.

The Black Barn field was ready for haying and T was out there astride the newly acquired old tractor, his bare back bronzed, the sharp blade of the mower cutting a clean swarth so, without a pause, the cycle was beginning again.

'I'll be up soon,' he promised, which would mean sometime after dark. 'When all the hay is in, we'll finish the conservatory.'

I picked up a handful of hay and smiled, for after the hay-making there would be straw-carting.

* * *

Our young sheepdog, Jill, proved a willing pupil. She had the most trusting eyes, and her shining long hair rippled in the sunshine, making her look bigger than she was, but should you pick her up, there was beneath those silken locks a tiny frame. She, Nicky and Roddy slept in the kennel at night, but were allowed in the house by day. Roddy would head for the nearest comfortable carpet (no lying on furniture allowed), but to begin with Jill, with her collie nature, was too timid to come in; she usually preferred being out of doors.

One morning in late July I found her outside the back door alternately staggering as if she was drunk and standing rigid on all four legs; froth was foaming out of the corners of her mouth. She was obviously seriously ill. The vet quickly diagnosed my fear: strychnine poisoning - and her life was in peril. The poison must have been laid by some careless person as a bait, probably intended for foxes, somewhere within the vicinity. Any stimulus would heighten the risk of further convulsions and possibly respiratory paralysis, and with a highly-strung breed like a collie, even the slightest bit of outside excitement could make the condition worse. There was no antidote; she would be given sedatives and placed in a totally dark, quiet room. Only time would tell if she would pull through.

Twenty-two hours later, she had recovered and returned home, to our enormous relief.

Our hopes for a good market for the lambs proved futile. Our first batch of fat lambs fetched less than they would have done two years before, since when galloping inflation of nearly 25%, (the second-highest since records began in 1750, and the highest since 1800), had led to soaring costs of fodder, labour and machinery. Petrol prices increased by nearly 70% in that year.

T soon found another way.

One of the advantages of working with sheep was the improvement of the condition of my hands, for no matter what the weather or the work the lanolin that secretes from their sebaceous glands kept my hands soft and smooth and my finger nails growing without any blemishes. Sometimes there would be so much of this 'wool wax' or 'wool grease' that I would have to use a towel to wipe off the excess. Of course, during the dire weather of the early weeks I was invariably wearing gloves and didn't gain the benefit of lanolin.

By the autumn, our first batch of one hundred lambs were despatched to Ashford market. It was not long before T decided he could make more money from the lambs by selling them from home instead of in the market. Not to another farmer or a butcher, mind you, but by taking them to the slaughter house himself, and fetching the hung carcases home a few days later. Occasionally, I was commandeered to collect them – in my newspaper van, of course.

T then butchered them at home, sometimes lying them in the bath until he was ready to proceed. I'm not sure which I liked less – collecting them from the abattoir or having them in what was meant to be my bath. Where he learnt the cutting skill from, I don't know, but soon he had them jointed, and put into packs of chops, loin, leg, shoulder, and neck.

Next, they had to be advertised, and after a few had been sold this way,

I scripted a new ad: *'Once people have tasted our lamb, they come back for more. It is fresh, tender, and reasonably priced. Pop one in your freezer soon. Tel Wadhurst 3464.'* The price for the advert was £1.62p, and the date was October 6, 1975. While not doing away entirely with the local markets a fair number were sold this way.

* * *

T decided to upgrade the old solid-fuel Rayburn with a second-hand oil-burning Aga. Even with Tim on hand to help him lift it he had not bargained for its weight; it was very, very heavy. It was also extremely difficult to assemble, and when its door was opened the main oven strewed piles of polystyrene beans all over the kitchen floor. I left them to it and went off to look round the flock, loving as always, the view across to the beechy toll, the full green of summer beginning to give way to autumn colours. As I walked round the perimeter of the 18-acre field I gazed below me where a few garlands of hops not yet harvested hung like pendulums. Walking back up the track I diverted into the band of trees, the ground still soft from last year's beech nuts, across the home paddock and into the kitchen – where the sight before me was of T and Tim leaning back triumphantly against the newly installed Aga. Now all we had to do was light it. Easier said than done! In time, it proved a boon.

* * *

As autumn approached so we began preparing horses for the coming season. Like the lambing, I prayed it would be a great deal better than last spring. At least the weather had improved; that dreadful rain and snow had morphed into a summer heatwave. I had recovered from my bad fall (though these days I have a distinctly creaky neck.) Luckily, such serious falls are relatively rare, and in the normal course of events, it is just as easy to be hurt when off a horse as on it.

Lay people often think of falling off as being the most dangerous part of riding but all too often it is while dealing with horses on the ground that mishaps happen. One time, I was loading our cob, Toby, into the trailer after an outing somewhere. He went in all right, but just as I had the rear ramp lifted half way up, he shot out backwards thrusting the ramp down on me with my thigh pinned by it and half a ton of horse on top. I truly thought I had broken my femur and that would put me out of the whole forthcoming racing season. Remarkably, it was only badly bruised – but to this day I carry an indentation across it – and ever since I have always stood to the side of a ramp rather than behind it. There is usually a back bar, too, but even with that, I don't take chances.

On another occasion, again when I was in my twenties, T and I were out riding along one of the Bayham Estate old carriageways; in late spring there is no finer place for a resplendent show of rhododendrons but this was still January.

We pulled up after a nice canter, both horses feeling well, when the one ahead lashed out and at full length, with his heels in the air, caught me on the forearm just below the elbow. Within moments a sharp point protruded through my sweater. I was in agony. A broken arm. And the point-to-point season, with its accompanying hopes and dreams, about to begin.

At the hospital, the A&E doctor looked at it, and said, 'Mrs T, I think it is broken,' at which point, with his mere confirmation, I rather pathetically burst into tears, and headed off to the x-ray department.

At length, with the x-ray taken, the doctor called me back in. 'Mrs T,' he said, looking me straight in the eye, 'you have very strong bones.' Again, I had got away with bad bruising and only 24 hours in a sling instead of six weeks in plaster.

Without doubt, the luckiest escape for two of our horses, my stepson and myself, came in the early hours at the end of 1975. I was heading off for a longed-for visit to hunt in the Shires, considered the crème de la crème, courtesy of belonging to the Melton Hunt Club. Tim, still a schoolboy, was coming along, too. One of the fun aspects of getting to know him had been teaching him to ride, and that treasured day when he came home with a large silver trophy, won aboard the family cob Toby. He was not yet riding thoroughbreds or hunting but was happy to help me on this trip, reading the map, plying the tea and sandwiches and being just plain good company.

The alarm rang shrilly at 3am. I had been half awaiting it for a couple of hours, concerned lest it failed to work and so thwart my trip. I stirred into heavy-eyed action, after one more mental check: soup ready, sandwiches cut, flask filled (necessary in this cold weather), hunting stock ironed, boots polished, horses plaited, tack cleaned and ready, map and directions – and that precious Melton Hunt Club ticket entitling me to a day with the Cottesmore on Tuesday December 15, 1975. It was cold and frosty in the south-east, but racing at Leicester the previous day had been free of fog and frost, so, with care and using main roads, I reasoned I could get there safely.

Before long the ageing Rough Scot and his younger companion, Romeo, were ready for loading. The old grey walked quietly into the narrow, dark trailer opening but the youngster had other ideas. Nothing would induce him to go in. Beginnings of fog came down masking the bright moon that had made the frost glisten. We tried every trick in the book in vain. The clock moved round to 4.30am. I had allowed more than ample time to combat the frost and fog before reaching the clear weather north of London.

'It's no use, we'll never get there,' I said in frustration. 'We'll take the other one – quick, let's swap the bandages.'

Good old Log, a couple of years junior to Scotty, ate a few oats out of my hand while Tim swapped knee pads and bandages then, unplaited and ungroomed, he walked up the ramp like a lamb and ten minutes later we were off. It was a slow, careful journey with the frost sparkling on the edges where the grit had not reached.

'We'll stick to the main roads all the way,' I repeated. The fog had cleared but the stretch of road we were now on between the towns of Tunbridge Wells and Tonbridge, appeared not to have been gritted. Cautiously I changed into third for a slight downhill slope; the horses, seasoned travellers, had not stirred. Both good hunters who had always qualified properly, I guessed they would take to Leicestershire well, and I looked forward to it eagerly.

Suddenly, the trailer began to sway, not in a normal way but pulling – sliding – to the right. With sinking stomach, I realised we had hit ice.

As the trailer swayed, so the two horses swayed with it, increasing the movement alarmingly (like a child on a swing). By now we were snaking across both lanes of the road; the one thing I knew not to do was brake. But to 'accelerate out of it' would have taken great courage. Events overtook us: Bang. Jolt. I saw a lamp post loom, as the trailer turned over, hit the kerb and skidded with sickening force. The driver's door flew open and the momentum threw me out, (seat belts weren't even fitted), into the path of the jack-knifing trailer. It came slowly to rest against my ankle, pinning me between Land Rover and trailer. For a second there was an eerie silence. Then the horses started struggling.

Tim ran straight round to the back of the overturned trailer, crawled through the jagged metal, gingerly over the horses to reach their heads where he firmly held the head of the more distressed one, Log. Then he started yelling, 'Anne, come ON!!' unaware that I was pinned helplessly between the two vehicles. It was still dark. I looked up the slope and saw the early morning milk tanker approaching. Its headlights picked out the black road. Supposing the same thing happened to him – I would be jam, and shuddered, it was the most frightening moment of the whole ordeal.

But the driver had seen the situation, overshot rather than braked, and came back. It took four men and a crowbar to free me with, miraculously, no more than a bruised ankle. Even more miraculously the horses, the winners between them of 28 races and loving their hunting too, were eventually freed, cut, bleeding, very, very dazed but alive and not in danger.

Rough Scot was the first horse to be rescued, by the firemen who were much braver than the various other people there; he had a nasty gash to a hind pastern but not so serious as to need stitching. After his memorable career it would have been tragic had he been killed.

Log lay there. Fearing his back might be broken the vet lifted his tail, whereupon the old horse kicked him – no damage there, then! More than anything he was in shock, and once he was able to get up there wasn't a scratch on him. Another miracle.

The episode was a salutary lesson. I thought, mistakenly, that if we were careful enough, we could get out of the tricky South-East and up to the Shires. The Police were sympathetic. As they gritted the road by hand themselves, not waiting for the council to come, one of them told me a trailer was the worst possible type of vehicle to have on ice.

Most articulated vehicles are fitted with anti-jack-knifing devices and police experts consider long-distance lorry drivers generally to be the knights of the road, (so do I,) but the casual caravan or horse-trailer driver is probably in possession of the most lethal type of vehicle on ice of all.

Most skid accidents are caused in the first place by a lack of observation of prevailing road conditions and too much acceleration, worsened by fierce braking and coarse steering. To correct a skid the driver must take his foot off the accelerator, but not brake, and steer gently into the skid when the back should slowly correct itself.

'But,' a Sussex Police Head Quarters Accident Prevention Officer told me later, 'once a caravan or trailer is on ice the weight of the trailer pushes forward treacherously and is uncontrollable; there is virtually nothing the driver can do.'

He added, 'Black ice is exactly what it says – it is unidentifiable until you are on it.'

So even if you have generally reduced speed in frosty conditions, black ice may still lurk to catch out the unwary.

Incidentally, I was told one should not confine skid sense to wintry conditions. Statistics show that there are more skid accidents in the summer when there is a shower of rain after a long dry spell and the roads are exceptionally greasy.

But to the trailer driver in winter there is only one piece of advice: if it is icy, do not venture out, however much you have been looking forward to the occasion. You and your innocent horses may end with no occasion at all.

Only ten days after this mishap, a momentous Act of Parliament took effect.

Riding Under Rules

On December 29th, 1975 the Sex Discrimination Act passed into English law. Apart from myriad more important female issues, women could in one swoop suddenly ride, with equal status, against men under National Hunt Rules; no gentle introduction via hunter-chasing, no ladies only races. On January 19th 1976 the Jockey Club announced it would be seeking further clarification and consultations. The next day it was announced that women could apply for professional or amateur NH licences in the same way as men. One week later, on January 27th, six women arrived at Portman Square to be interviewed by the licensing stewards. In the past, for a man to apply, he had only to send in an application by post accompanied by a reference from a trainer.

First in was Mrs Sue Horton and 8 ½ minutes later, facing much fanfare and flashing of press cameras, she emerged waving her new licence. Sue was a stunning blonde bombshell and one of the most competent lady riders of any era. She rode exceptionally short and gave the inside away to no-one. Once, thinking I was hugging the fence flag, she popped her horse through between it and me as if the gap was as wide as the Nile. As Sue Aston she was leading lady point-to-point rider five times and had ridden her first winner at 14 years old before the minimum age came in. Sadly, Sue died at the age of 43 in April 1986 when she was found dead in her car in the garage of her Wiltshire home. It was found that she had dropped off to sleep with the engine running and was overcome by fumes. The Coroner's verdict was accidental death by carbon monoxide poisoning.

Muriel Naughton and the Thorne twins, Jane and Diana, were next to receive their licences, but the 'mature' Marie Tinkler and Shelagh French were told they would have to have medical examinations. Marie, who was 51 and an able point-to-point rider, 'failed'; her trainer husband Colin raged at the effrontery, claiming his wife was twice as fit and stronger than he but, in the end, she chose not to fight.

Shelagh French, younger by four years, was passed, to the relief of all who knew her. She dead-heated with another lady rider in a Fontwell novice hunter-chase at the end of that season, becoming the joint sixth woman to win; nine races were won by lady riders that first half season, three of them by Gillian Fortescue Thomas, a former donkey Grand National winner who went on to become a professional racing driver for Ford.

Within hours of the granting of the first ladies' permits, the Jockeys' Association was up in arms about the "threat to their members' livelihoods".

They demanded that amateurs should have ridden in 75 amateur races (excluding point-to-points) before they were allowed to ride against professionals. In an almost indecently hasty reaction, the Association claimed that their aim was to protect the earning capacity of the professionals and their safety. They insisted that a riding fee should be paid for these amateurs, to go into a fund to ensure adequate insurance cover.

Resentment of amateurs by professionals had long been prevalent in racing and the Jockey Club had already taken steps to ensure that a successful amateur did not "pinch" rides from professionals. In the old days they would politely ask such riders either to turn professional or to withdraw discreetly from the scene. Later they ruled that after an amateur had ridden in 75 races against professionals, the owner would have to pay a full riding fee – this did not, of course, go to the amateur, but is swallowed up in the administrative costs of racing. The only exception was where the amateur rides his own horse or one belonging to his wife, parents or children.

One of my contemporaries, Nicky Batchelor, who lived with her boyfriend, a Kent fruit farmer Roger Ledger, was interviewed by the Stewards and they asked her, as she was an amateur, what means she had for keeping herself. The result was that she and Roger quickly got married. Different days.

Another momentous occurrence that January concerned great speed and grace: the first commercial flight of the magnificent supersonic Concorde. She was the most beautiful aeroplane with state-of-the-art technology in a joint Anglo-Franco enterprise – but in July 2000 a piece of debris on the runway and too much fuel in the aircraft's tank at Orly airport did for her; her sister plane flew for another three years but falling passenger numbers led to her withdrawal from service in 2003, just 27 years after she began commercial operations.

There was a huge sense of anticipation and excitement at the prospect of riding under Rules and within a matter of days I, too, had my licence and three weeks after the first lady to ride under rules, I found myself lining up in front of the tapes. Exciting times! We still had the nicely bred but ageing Log, fully recovered from his trailer jack-knife experience. He was something of a 'has-been' but a safe conveyance, and latterly he was usually blinkered. Nevertheless, he was not likely to disgrace himself – or his lady rider.

It was with even more nerves than usual that on February 21st 1976 we set off for Lingfield, kitbag packed, saddle polished, where I was to ride in the RE Sassoon Memorial Hunters Chase. Lingfield today is better known as an all-year-round all-weather flat course complete with Derby Trial, a good practice for Epsom because of its sweeping left-handed downhill gradient. Its NH course on grass continues to hold fixtures during the winter season, although the chase fences no longer have the mature growing hedges that formed attractive wings. There also used to be a point-to-point course tucked within the far end.

There was no changing room for lady riders, there simply hadn't been time to organise a separate facility. This was the same countrywide that first year or two: it could be a hastily brought in caravan, a ladies WC, or on this occasion, a curtained off section of the first aid room, disconcerting for injured male jockeys and lady riders alike, equally needing privacy.

Once changed, I bumped into my hero, Fred Winter. A man of a few well-chosen words, he advised me to 'keep cool, use your head – and enjoy yourself afterwards.'

Log cantered quietly down to the start with our 11 rivals and for the first time I faced a starting tape (point-to-points are started by flag), and bigger fences. But Log was an old pro, and although well outclassed in the race he gave me a good safe ride to come sixth of eight finishers. Two runners had fallen but Log made just one mistake that shot me up his neck leading Fred Winter to enquire afterwards, with that twinkle in his eye, 'and what were you whispering into his ear?'

The race was won by Andrew Wates on Dusky May, beating the Nicky Henderson-ridden, Fred Winter-trained favourite Into View.

* * *

In another six weeks our second lambing season was due to start, and all the usual tasks were in process. What had we learnt from that disastrous first year? Surely nothing could be as bad as that again, could it? A great deal of knowledge had been acquired and, for one, orphan lambs were to become almost a thing of the past, thanks to the successful skinning and fostering. Also, the weather was better – considerably.

Certainly, I felt less pressure in the fields, and was able to get in some much better rides – with some good luck for Roman Receipt aka Romeo – in addition to my first ride under National Hunt Rules. That spring the ground was often recorded as hard, which evidently suited Romeo.

It was a typical Easter Monday point-to-point at Heathfield with large crowds and small fields. Large hampers and small children abounded and as usual a number of cars had distinguishing flags (or dusters) flying from them. Significantly, there was also a specific marker flag out on the course, staked on a bend in the track.

The ladies race as usual was a feature. Just three of us went to post; a pretty blonde was on the favourite owned by the Master. Roman Receipt was seven and, although he had run in a couple of men's races this was my first on him since the dreadful fall at the end of the previous season, so I was happy to settle him in behind the other two. But we had only crossed four fences, and reached the point where the course turns left by a flag into a dip before rising up and bearing right-handed again, that to my astonishment I saw both the other riders gallop the wrong side of the flag. Neither of them pulled up. That meant I could continue to take a nice lead off them – to negotiate one and a half circuits solo would be a big ask for a young horse.

At the end of the first circuit one of them pulled up but the favourite continued. Thank-you! Now the open ditch and last bend were negotiated. Just the drop fence and two in the straight remained. After the drop I let Romeo close the gap but still didn't hustle him, for there was no need. The favourite 'won' by perhaps a couple of lengths. The girl was congratulated until the inevitable stewards' enquiry was announced. I did feel sorry for her because she had no idea of what had happened and what should have been her most exciting moment, her first win, was dashed. The huntsman suggested she should be allowed to keep the race. But disqualification was inevitable.

Five days later we met again, at the West Kent meeting at Ightham. Oh, if ours had been a betting stable could we ever have made a killing. Of all the rides in my career, this was the one above all others when a handsome bet could have been justified.

Because, naturally, the other horse was favourite. Hadn't he 'beaten' mine already, for sure. This time we had two rivals, but on the second circuit the favourite and I pulled clear of them. My fellow nipped through on the inside at the last bend to take the lead, increasing it to a couple of lengths over the last two fences.

This time there was no dubiety about the winner – or his worthiness.

Rough Scot was to have two runs that year, 1976. At 14, he was ageing, and he was more laid back than ever so that he would now not only plod round the paddock before a race, but also, he wouldn't deign to walk at all down at the start. But come the line-up and the drop of the flag, he took hold of the bit and was off, doing what he loved best, point-to-pointing.

The old boy was fit and well. He couldn't go the pace in a 'men's' race at Aldington, finishing sixth just behind another South East stalwart, the Hackings' Red Cast who was a year older. He had won many open races and hunter chases in his prime under Robert Hacking.

Next for Rough Scot was his favourite Heathfield where he was to contest the Eridge Hunt Members Race on Easter Monday.

Since 1967, nine years before the Sex Discrimination Act, women had been allowed, at the discretion of the organising committee, to contend just one race against men, and that was their own hunt race. At the time, only three hunts (out of some 170 or so) had declined to allow women to participate; the Eridge was one of them – and at the time I was their only lady rider. This was commented on by the local paper, the *Kent and Sussex Courier*. In its preview of the meeting, it had a paragraph headed **NO LADIES** and read: *'Eridge has not allowed ladies to enter the members' race as they can by rule this season. It can hardly be supposed that the Eridge men are frightened to race against the ladies but what other reason can there be?'*

Two years later, when the organisers had relented, the same newspaper blazed: *'ANNE BEATS MEN IN MEMBERS' RACE.'*

Not the sort of headline one would see today!

That occasion was memorable and a fine achievement from my mount, because instead of the ultra-reliable Rough Scot, I was riding Margaret's home bred Tangled Web (by Tangle out of Royal Catch.) She was young, raw – and talented. She was learning as she went around, feeling strong but a mistake at the second last caused me to lose my stirrup irons. That didn't stop her. She was so fit and well that on she galloped, jumped the last well clear to win convincingly, and then, as I had no irons, I couldn't pull her up. This meant spectators, who had spread out onto the course with the race over, had to scatter for cover as we careened on towards them. The magic of that day was that Margaret had bred both the horse and the jockey. Sadly, Tangled Web was to suffer tendon trouble and her true worth never materialised; instead, she swelled Margaret's growing brood mare enterprise, breeding Spider Man, who won the Lionel Vic Memorial Gold Cup at Newbury, when trained by Mrs Betty Kennard for his new owner.

Tangled Web – a homebred mare of infinite promise, but blighted by tendon trouble.

Another home-bred was an exceptionally good-looking chestnut with such a perfect, floating stride that Lady March, who hosted the international dressage championships at Goodwood House for twenty-one years, came to see him. Sadly, a few days later, he contracted colic, was led round and round the small paddock to try and ease the problem, but died in heart-rending pain. He was four years old and on the cusp of what should have been an idyllic life.

Now, for what was to be Rough Scot's last race in 1976, he had to hump 12st 7lbs (about four and a half stone of that made up in dead weight) – but he galloped and jumped and nipped his way round the Heathfield corners and up that final hill of his familiar course – and into honourable retirement by winning his sixteenth race.

Seven years later, Margaret hosted a 21st birthday party for him attended by old fans and rival jockeys alike. The star arrived at the patio of the house ridden by George Adams, Rough Scot resplendent in his old paddock sheet in time for the cutting the cake ceremony – and a decent handful of carrots for him.

Rough Scot's 21ˢᵗ birthday party, 1983, owner Margaret Holland, right; George Adams in the saddle; he originally came as farm manager but soon found himself learning a lot about horses.

A horse that quickens when it sees a fence and attacks it with gusto, soaring over on a perfect stride, and when that same horse does it eighteen times in the course of one race and gallops clear of his rivals to the line – that gives a matchless sensation for the rider.

I was very lucky with Rough Scot, the iron grey with the lion heart, a relentless galloper who didn't do off days. When Tarkaotter was fit and well, he was like a lean, mean racing machine and I dreamed the dream on him.

* * *

Ascot Sales used to be a happy hunting ground for us, and on the whole, we had been lucky with our modestly-priced purchases. But now here was the vet talking.

'I'm afraid it hasn't worked. We'll have to operate again.'

I listened with misgivings and sinking heart to the vet. Our lovely mare who had shown exceptional promise, winning by a 'street' in only her second race the year before, was diagnosed with navicular, a degenerative condition of a small bone of that name within a horse's hoof. It makes a horse chronically and increasingly lame with the possibility of the hoof eventually crumbling away.

I thought back to the day we bought her at the old Ascot Sales. We were selling a horse and not really looking to buy. But there she was, stabled next to ours, a big, strapping four-year-old chestnut mare called Ebnal Goddess. She had won three times in the show ring and it was evident why as I saw plenty of her trotting up and down for viewers; I enjoyed chatting to her vendors in quiet spells. They had travelled down from Yorkshire and were surprised but genuinely pleased when we bought her.

At home Heidi, as we nicknamed her, was fairly green, as one would expect of a four-year-old, but she took to hunting and enjoyed hacking through the woods. One day in the new year, when like all thoroughbreds she had had her official birthday on January 1, I took her for a canter up a long, green stretch of Eridge Park. It was between Saxonbury Woods on one side and Whitehill – that special place – on the other. As I wound my way down Whitehill's unspoilt heathland interspersed with ancient trees, I marvelled as ever at the whole beautifully-clothed hill. We crossed over the stream by an old stone bridge at the bottom and set off to canter up the long sward of lush grass beyond. Suddenly, as we were midway through the canter, I felt the most amazing metamorphosis taking place to the magnificent animal beneath me, stretching those long legs forward and devouring the ground. Gone was the gangly schoolgirl, here was the real deal, a transformation. It was a most exciting moment – she was now a racehorse and we both knew it, so in a way it was no surprise that she won so easily on only her second appearance.

Now here was the vet saying she would have to be de-nerved.

I turned away.

Why does it happen to the good ones? Chestnut mares, perhaps justifiably, have a reputation for being hot-headed, difficult and wayward. But like the little girl with the curl in the middle of the forehead, when they are good, they are very, very good.

Unlike another mare I purchased at Ascot Sales. It was when they held a show the previous day and she had come second. Not only was she good looking but she had a pedigree bursting with good point-to-point form on both sides. I paid £1,000 for her and thought I had the bargain of the sale. She was also four and so, like Heidi, should have been unspoilt.

But all too soon I found out differently. She bit – catching me painfully on my backside once – she kicked, but worst of all she reared. It is the worst vice a horse can have, but hers was more sinister than that: she looked for the nearest solid object, a wall, a tree, and backed up to it before rearing, trying to crush her rider.

Because I felt she was worth a try I sent her to renowned Sussex horseman Roy Trigg to see if he could sort her out. Apparently, she quickly broke 12 bridles (I'm not quite sure how), but she returned well-mannered so I tried again. Unfortunately, soon after that we went away on holiday, and when we returned, she had reverted to her old ways. Back she went to Ascot Sales, but this time with no reserve, no vet's certificate, and as 'the property of a lady,' a euphemism for the owner not wanting to have anything to do with her. I think she fetched 300 guineas.

Neither mares nor youngsters were usual purchases for T and me. More the norm was an older horse, with form in the distant past but evidently with some problems now: the horse might have been fired, perhaps, scars indicating an operation for past tendon trouble, or the form book showed that he wore blinkers, indicating that he might be ungenuine. These sorts could often be picked up for relatively small money but almost to a horse they won at least one race for us. Hacking through the woods of East Sussex, hunting behind the Eridge hounds, being treated as a special individual in part of a small, close family instead of a number in a long string and getting bored with the same old, same old, all of these factors saw to their transformation.

* * *

I was so, so lucky in my career in that I never had a horse killed. Rough Scot virtually never made a jumping error, being such a compact horse that even at full gallop he could put himself right – in contrast to Master Jock! Margaret lost one; she had bought the only full sister to Master Jock and Rough Scot, a grey called Summit Of Blue. She won her maiden by a distance for Guy Peate at Charing, gave Patsy a few rides in Ladies races, and then headed off to Folkestone for a hunter chase. United Hunts' day at Folkestone was an annual trip where all six races on the card were hunter chases, (Folkestone closed in 2012, and the meeting was transferred to Fontwell.) Folkestone was always a great day out, the more so on the occasions Margaret had a runner; she had once had a horse beaten by a short head. This was Chasewood, an older half-brother to Rough Scot et al, who had given Margaret her first point-to-point winner.

Summit Of Blue had already won, she was the only full sister to the multiple winning brothers, (there were others, that Margaret could not afford to buy after Master Jock and Rough Scot had done so well,) and the intention was to put her in foal and continue the dynasty. But for some reason that day at Folkestone, Summit Of Blue 'missed out' a fence so completely that she demolished it – and broke her back. Guy was seriously injured and a few short years later, aged in his early forties, he developed stomach cancer and died, leaving a widow and five young children. Margaret provided a beautiful silver Armada dish as a trophy for a race at Folkestone, (and now presented at Fontwell) that was renamed the Guy Peate Memorial. Guy had been a big part of our lives.

Guy Peate was a big part of our lives.

On one occasion I had a horse die (as opposed to killed or put down), and that, too, was at Folkestone. It was in a hurdle race, a spare ride, probably ten years later. Bred to win a Derby, his purple blood had failed to come up trumps on the racecourse. It was somewhat alarming when riding him out first for the trainer on the former Lewes racecourse because a Land Rover had to be revved up and driven behind him to make him start. In the race I decided to try and let him enjoy himself, and let him go off in the lead, galloping and jumping for fun. There we stayed until a loose horse veered across us and his chance was gone; soon after I pulled him up, turned, and started walking back. Suddenly I felt his hind legs give way; he walked another stride and it happened again so I swiftly jumped off. This time he did not recover but collapsed to the ground. Plainly he was dying, and so I sat by his head, stroking him and talking to him for the few minutes it took.

* * *

The advent of women in NH racing was to lead to a couple of changes. Before the Sex Discrimination Act there had been no lower age limit for men, but females could not ride in a point-to-point until they were 18; a compromise was reached with the across-the-board minimum age of 16. The other was the introduction of A and B amateur licences in July 1977; before then amateurs could ride in almost all races. The concern was put about that inexperienced women might cause trouble if racing against professional jockeys (all male) though in truth, with years of point-to-point experience behind most lady riders, inexperience was just as likely to be found amongst novice men. The A licence restricted novices of either sex to amateur riders' races only, and only when they had notched up 15 completed rides under Rules or finished in the first three on that number of occasions in point-to-points could they gain a B licence enabling them to ride against professionals.

But to begin with there was no such restriction, and before long I found myself enjoying hurdle racing as well as chasing, so we set about looking for a suitable horse. King's Rhapsody was yet another 'cast off': blinkered, fired, and decidedly out of love with the game. He had never been first past the post but had been promoted on disqualification of a winner on the Flat, so he was ineligible for maidens.

He was advertised for sale in Warwickshire in *Horse and Hound*, a distance so far from Sussex that we drove up with the trailer. We greeted the vendors on arrival with the words that the trailer was not to be taken as an indication that we would buy the horse! But buy him we did - Margaret parting with £725 for him. The couple, David and Jane Lowe, became lifelong friends and David became my son's godfather. In the early 1980s they owned and had bred Out Of The Gloom, who proved a top-class hurdler, trained by Reg Hollinshead. He won the Fighting Fifth hurdle race at Newcastle, a Champion Hurdle indicator, and later that year they gave a splendid celebration party.

Neat and athletic, a dark brown, King's Rhapsody became one of my favourites – with good reason. He was easy to do at home and to train and although he could pop in the odd buck when feeling well, they were not the unseating variety. He was kind and well-behaved – a proper gent. He looked an ideal candidate to progress my hurdling aspirations.

A first run at Plumpton left him mired in the mud.

King's Rhapsody at Plumpton; Nicky Ledger is on the left.

Then he was unsound. For four months. It was one of those frustrating, intermittent lameness's where it is impossible to pinpoint the source; x-rays, veterinary inspections and farrier's probing all failed to find the reason. I was able to keep exercising him on soft ground, which kept him semi-fit.

Then he was diagnosed with ringbone.

After just one race, were we to lose him? The problem could either settle or worsen.

Suddenly, however, the occasional lameness became acute. This time his foot was flaming hot. More probing and whoosh – pus shot out from his fetlock (equivalent of a wrist) as if from a volcano. You could almost feel the release of tension (nothing to do with the ringbone). It had been brewing up all that time, probably caused by a piece of grit that had worked its way under his shoe and meandered around his foot, getting more and more irritable until it had wound its way upwards into his heel and eventually come to a head at a point soft enough to allow it to push its way through to exit.

There was just enough left of the season to have me pouring over the entry books; there was a 2 ¾-mile hurdle at Fontwell in early June; he could have a prep race in a selling hurdle race at Stratford before that. A seller? But we don't bet! We scoured the Jockey Club Rule Book to learn everything we could. As it was to be a warm up race to get him ready for Fontwell, we decided we might as well go anyway.

First, I had to get him fit enough. Luckily, he was a light, active sort, and a trip down to Camber Sands near Rye, where I was able to work him for nearly two miles – as well as let him enjoy a paddle in the sea, ideal for his recently suffering foot – left him spot on.

So once more the old trailer headed off from East Sussex, this time in a May heat wave, all the way to Stratford-on-Avon – where hordes of tourists threatened to delay us – and reached the course just in time. On the way up Margaret joked that she would buy us all dinner in a smart restaurant if we won. If we won, we laughed back, we'd likely be on fish and chips because the race was a seller. (A seller is just that – the winner is put up for auction immediately after the race; the owner is allowed to bid and may therefore buy his or her own horse back; a certain amount of the sale price goes to the racecourse. It generally attracts only very modest horses, or those who have 'lost their way', and because an owner may end up buying back his own horse, betting is often the answer to making any money from a win.)

King's starting price with the bookmakers was 20-1, with a couple of others at even longer odds. Not surprisingly I was the only lady rider – it was 1977 and therefore the first full season in which women could participate, still making us something of a novelty under Rules – and the rest were professionals. The favourite was Knave of Hearts, ridden by Ron Hyett for Martin Tate, and B.R. – Bob – Davies was on the second favourite, Kath's Bounty.

King's dark coat gleamed in the May sunshine. He looked a picture.

It was a glorious evening and ours was the first race. Facilities for women were minimal; here there was a small caravan parked on the concrete concourse vaguely in the vicinity of the main stand, and the sun glared on to it, and reflected up off the concrete. It was like a sauna. After the race and sitting on the steps I hailed a passing policeman and asked him to help me pull off my boots – all in a copper's day's work! There may have been water in the caravan but I don't remember it, and I'm sure there wasn't a valet. Anyway, I found my way to the weighing room carrying my specially weighted 21lb racing saddle – the one that Bob Champion saw me with once and remarked that it looked like an armchair.

Soon we were cantering down to the start. One of the professional jockeys called over to me, 'You'll stay on the wide outside, dear, won't you?' Gospel truth!

Soon up went the tapes and off went King and I straight to the front, to let him enjoy himself and bowl along. I can still imagine the jockeys' smirks behind me as they let me blaze the trail.

We rounded the final bend with one more to jump. Could hear the pounding hoof beats getting ever closer and fully expected to be 'swallowed up' any second – but it didn't happen. All the way to the line we maintained our lead.

Instead of euphoria, my first reaction was, 'Oh my God, it's a seller.' The celebrations would come later. Margaret had had a tenner on at 30-1 on the Tote.

The auction seemed interminable. Just as it looked as if we may get away with no bid the auctioneer said, 'Nice ride for a lady.' Immediately someone bid. Margaret countered.

This may have gone on, perhaps, a couple of times, and then we had bought our own horse. Now everything sank in. We'd WON! Mum's first winner under Rules (many years after that short head second with Chasewood at Folkestone); ridden by her daughter; against professional jockeys. We were all on cloud nine. A humble seller it may have been. To us it might just as well have been the Grand National. The dinner was good, too. A couple of weeks later what I strongly suspected was confirmed, which means that my son George, born the following January, 1978, has ridden a winner.

King's Rhapsody wins the Dealers Selling Handicap Hurdle race,
Stratford-upon-Avon, May, 1977. Photo Bernard Parkin

New Challenges

Remarkably, Roman Receipt, on whom I'd had that dreadful fall and then the two little wins the following year, was to enter my life again. He had been sold after I had 'retired' from racing after the birth of our son, George.

What a January night that was. It had started when I chased after a ram that had escaped but, being so top-heavy, I promptly fell over. That night, T quickly went off to sleep but I felt a few twangs; at two days overdue, motherhood was imminent. Eventually, I crept downstairs and rang the hospital. Come in right away, they said. I went upstairs to wake T. Slowly, still in dressing gown, he came down and put the kettle on the Aga. Fair play, he was trying to keep cool and calm. But the pains were now frequent. At length, I persuaded him that I really did have to go. The dark night was illuminated by bright stars above and sparkling frost underfoot. Slowly we made our way out of Dewhurst Lane and joined the main road heading for Crowborough Cottage Hospital, and its six-bedded maternity unit. The trouble then was that T didn't know the town and I had to try and direct him, easier said than done between gasps. Once at the hospital, my waters promptly broke on the doorstep. I never made it to the delivery room, but was well attended to in the nearest room and at one in the morning George was born.

That night, it snowed so hard that had birth come a day later it would have been to hospital by tractor – or a home birth. I suppose T had gained plenty of experience with the lambs and would have managed!

Motherhood was amazing and I loved it. Naturally, I did not race in the February to May months that then comprised the whole point-to-point season, but I was soon riding out, and I also went hunting before the end of the season. The main thing happening at Newlands, apart from tending the flock and the usual associated jobs, was that, with a new-born now in the family, we decided to upgrade to mains electricity. Gone were the days of the temperamental, noisy generator. It was certainly worth it. We also extended the cottage to make a good-sized bedroom above the existing single-story bathroom and kitchen.

One of the sadder things that happy year involved Robin Fane-Gladwin, with whom I had stayed on Exmoor after my bad fall at the end of our first year's lambing in 1975. She had moved there from East Sussex where she had been a well-known and popular figure in the hunting and horse world; she had also virtually brought up two children of, I think, her domestic helper and they were excellent riders. After my stay with her, T joined me in another visit to her pretty Exmoor cottage, log fire roaring, meal cooking. She went into the kitchen to make the gravy – and came back blotto. No remark was passed at the time, but a neighbour told me of her drinking problem.

I kept in occasional touch with her and in 1978 received a letter headed *Ward 29, Frenchay Hospital, Bristol. Dec 4th*.

My dearest Ann, T & Baby George,

Thank you so much for your welcome letter, you are obviously very out of date -!! I have been here for nearly 3 weeks with a terrible burn on my back, I slipped & fell backwards into the open fireplace & burnt my left shoulder & ½ my back, & was rushed here in an ambulance to the burns unit, where I am waiting for the skin to get right, before they can do a skin graft. I'm in considerable pain & discomfort & live on painkillers, they are peeling the skin off now & making it raw -! &I believe for the 1st few days after the graft its worse, I shall be here all over Xmas, & I'm feeling so low & depressed, your letter came at the right moment, before this happened I had been for 3 weeks to a London Nursing Home for a cure to the other illness, & was getting on fine, & then this had to happen, if there had been any doubts as to if I was cured before this horrific accident, there can be none now, this is a thing that will haunt me all my life. Whenever I think of it I try to be brave but the whole thing is so awful, sometimes I feel I shall never be right again. Luckily all the animals have been happily placed till I can return home, dogs, horse & sheep, & the house is shut up with Peggy going in to air it. Do

write again if you have time. I'm so glad Ann you have had some nice rides,
I saw Spider Man run on the television! Have you got an up to date photo
of George, I'd love to see one. Wonder if you've had any hunting, I've only
had 3 days, but maybe if I survive I'll get some spring hunting. This place is
terrifying with all the patients, almost gruesome. Give my love to Margaret
& Rex & lots to yourselves.

Rob xxx
Please write

I did better than that by visiting her instead. But a few short weeks later
T and I drove down to her funeral. It was a miserable affair. We were the
only ones, apart from her solicitor, Christopher Hall, who had travelled
down from her former lifelong home area, and there were just a handful
of other people in the bleak crematorium. It gave me a lasting aversion to
such places, and I much prefer services that celebrate a life in a traditional
English church.

In the autumn of 1978, I returned to the racing saddle for some hurdling on
King's Rhapsody. After our surprise win at Stratford-on-Avon, he had run at
Fontwell when quite well fancied, but another horse struck into one of his
hind legs and he was badly injured, resulting in several months box rest. I
didn't ride any horse again until George was a number of weeks old.

Now King's Rhapsody was fit again, and so was I, but the best we
managed was a distant third. One particularly memorable race was the
amateurs' hurdle that followed the Grand National at Aintree. Our chances
were as good as zero, as his price of 100-1 indicated, but in terms of
experience it was right up there with the best: the long, long haul up from
Sussex in the faithful trailer; staying overnight in the lads' hostel beside
the stables; riding out early next morning amongst horses who were due
to run in that afternoon's National – won for the first time by a Scottish-
trained horse, Rubstic. To enjoy the camaraderie with two or three other
lady riders in a ladies WC turned into our changing room; for a few
moments, it also offered refuge to Jenny Pitman, looking for escape from
the Press and an opportunity for a fag in a quiet place; trailing in last in the
race itself; and as we left to travel home, of the stands now empty, save for
a sea of white litter.

We had sold Roman Receipt to a novice rider in Kent. He had already
proved a reliable schoolmaster for a girl who worked for us, Jackie Taylor.
Originally, her mother had helped mine in the house when we lived in

Tunbridge Wells. When Mrs Taylor's horse-mad 14-year-old daughter discovered we had the stables at Frant, Jackie hopped on her bicycle and rode the three miles, including the notorious long, steep Frant Hill, and asked if she could work for us at week-ends and school holidays. She didn't ride but she was keen to learn not only how to ride but also all aspects of looking after horses, grooming, mucking out, cleaning tack. When she left school, she joined us and was a boon; and her reward, apart from enjoying riding out every day, was to have a ride on Roman Receipt in a point-to-point.

Eventually, wanting to earn more money, she went to work in a supermarket, where she earnt enough to buy a car and so on, but she pined to be among horses again, answered an advert, and found herself working for an East Anglian point-to-point stable. From there, she got to know and love life in and around Newmarket, met a red-haired flat jockey Bryn Crossley and married him in St Mark's Church, Broadwater Down, Tunbridge Wells. The marriage did not last, and in time Jaci, as she became known, married Richard Hills, from the Hills racing dynasty. Richard and his twin brother Michael were top-flight flat jockeys, and their father, Barry, a leading trainer in Lambourn. Richard and Jaci had a son, Patrick, who also became a flat jockey. Later in his career Richard and Jaci spent every winter in Dubai where Richard rode for Hamdam Al Maktoum until Richard retired in 2012 after 33 years in the saddle. Jaci continued to ride out for Sir Michael Stoute, look after her and Richard's stud a couple of miles out of Newmarket and enjoy their large dogs. It was while they were in Dubai that an Arab spelt her name as Jaci , and so she spelt it that way from then on.

Roman Receipt was set to continue his role as a schoolmaster after we sold him.

Roman Receipt was not a world-beater, but is part of the story.

In the spring of 1979 and with George a year old, it was generally assumed I would not be chasing, and that I had given up point-to-pointing, so when King's Rhapsody was tried steeplechasing, we put a lad up. One day, at a point-to-point in Kent, I was standing at the last fence watching the ladies race and as my former colleagues flew over it, a lump rose in my throat. I missed it.

A week later, an extraordinary thing happened. It was Easter Saturday and Roman Receipt ran in the first race at Charing for his new owner, but a stirrup leather broke after barely three-quarters of a mile. It happened he was also entered in the last race, but the owner had another horse in that as well. Would he like me to ride Romeo, I enquired? When the answer was yes, I had to borrow breeches, boots, helmet, whip, saddle – everything except the colours, in fact, and before I knew it, with no time for nerves, I was in the saddle and cantering to the start. We won the race, and I was back racing for a magical four more years. King's Rhapsody was part of that, giving me a win in a ladies race at good old Heathfield, and also finishing third in a chase at Fontwell. Eventually, I rode him in the Newmarket Town Plate, enroute to a new home in East Anglia, where he became an ideal schoolmaster for a girl starting out on her pointing career.

* * *

After my unexpected point-to-point come-back we acquired Mister Tack, previously fired and blinkered under NH Rules, for a modest sum at Ascot Sales in the autumn of 1980. A recession was on, unemployment was in the process of rising by 70%, and a number of IRA hunger strikers died during the year. In December John Lennon was murdered in New York, and one of two Radio Caroline pirate ships ran aground and sank. The commercial pop station was set up off shore to take on the BBC's broadcasting monopoly in 1964. There was many a time at Battle Abbey when various girls would find it on their radio transmitter dials, after earlier years of listening to Radio Luxembourg clandestinely under the bed clothes. I believe it was as a result of Caroline's success that the BBC introduced Radio 1.

Mister Tack proved a revelation, and he galloped and jumped to two memorable hat-tricks in consecutive years, 1981 and 1982, including some tingling duels against Jacksway (Clair Mair) at Parham, West Sussex; and two at Tweseldown, beating, firstly, Zarajeff (Jenny Pigeon, the first time that horse was beaten when completing a course), and next Housemistress (Rosemary Harper, later Henderson who was to finish fifth in the 1994 Grand National on Fiddlers Pike at 100-1).

Mister Tack beats Jacksway (Claire Mair) at the last at Parham, 1981

FEBRUARY 12 1982

HORSE and HOUND

EVERY FRIDAY 50p

I FREELY ADMIT THAT THE BEST OF MY FUN I OWE IT TO HORSE AND HOUND — WHYTE MELVILLE

Point-to-Pointing last Saturday

Mister Tack holds off Housemistress (Rosemary Harper) at Tweseldown, 1982. Zarajeff (Jenny Pigeon) was third, Horse and Hound cover

Mister Tack was a good horse, and had a massive buck; he got me off in the snow once in a field at home, and another time in full gallop (when it is unusual for a horse to buck.) His win at the Tickham meeting at Detling earned him qualification for the end-of-season ladies champion hunter chase at Chepstow, and that was another notable experience, for all that we pulled up in the race.

Mister Tack was a natural for hunting, and I took him off to the Mid-Surrey Farmers' Draghounds where he took to the big hedges with aplomb; the post-hunting tea and chatting was good, too, with people like Duggie Bunn and Edward Cazalet, as well as Philip Kindersley, who by then followed by car. Mister Tack was typical of the sort of horse, previously out of love with racing, who was sweetened up by hunting. It is not for every racehorse, one example being my first, Tarkaotter, who would refuse point blank to even walk over a log eighteen inches high out hunting – but give him a 4ft3in birch fence in a point-to-point, and it would be hard to find a better jumper. I would often take a horse out for the occasional day hunting even after it had qualified, just to keep it happy. Point-to-points quite often had a huntsman blow the 'gone away' on the horn as the starter's flag dropped, and that definitely encouraged a horse like Mister Tack.

In the outside world, 1981 was notable for the victory of Bob Champion on Aldaniti in the Grand National, the equally scintillating victory in the Derby of Shergar, subsequently kidnapped and shot by the IRA – and for the ill-fated marriage of Prince Charles to Lady Diana Spencer.

My toddler George ran a temperature of 102° for four days in January but was bouncing a few days later when he excitedly celebrated his third birthday, and was otherwise a healthy, vocal runabout. By lambing time, we now habitually took in a university veterinary student to give him or her first-hand experience of lambing. One year it was James Crowhurst who became an eminent Newmarket vet, and was nephew of Arnold Crowhurst who had advised us on Tarkaotter all those years before. And so, with a toddler in tow, my role on the farm lessened, even though Tim had now moved on, far away to what had been Southern Rhodesia, newly Zimbabwe, with his girlfriend, Jane. In time, he settled permanently in South Africa, married a girl from Botswana, and brought up a family of four, in addition to runing food and drink businesses.

Having given up working for the local paper shortly before George's birth, my freelance career was building up slowly but steadily with a number of magazines, and for the local radio, for whom I dictated point-to-point reports from the nearest public telephone box. I had also had my first full length book published, "They're Off!" The Story of the First Girl Jump Jockeys, with a foreword by the admirable Lord Oaksey.

John Oaksey was one of the greatest wordsmiths of his, or any era.

Perhaps best of all was his founding of the Injured Jockeys Fund in 1964 following racing falls to Paddy Farrell and Tim Brookshaw which left both jockeys permanently paralysed.

It is not just the high-profile jockeys with serious injuries who benefit; a beneficiary might not need accident-related help at all if a former licence holder has 'simply' fallen on hard times.

And even a lowly point-to-point or amateur rider from 50 years ago can receive help if in need, as I was most gratefully to discover when the IJF generously assisted towards a hip replacement in 2021.

Back in the 1980s, my principal work was for *Horse and Hound:* big horse shows like the South of England at Ardingly (1,000 words), and Kent County, both of them run over three days, in addition to a weekly column called Young Entry. This was an enjoyable job covering junior show-jumping across the whole of the southern half of England from East Anglia down to the West Country and across to south Wales; it involved not only big mileage but also numerous phone calls. The Midlands and the North was covered by a widow called Cynthia Muir, a dear lady, dedicated to her job but I especially remember her for saying that she just longed to be reunited with her husband one day. The column was dedicated to a mixed bunch of junior show-jumpers all with one goal: to qualify for the JA Championship at the Horse of the Year Show, then held at Wembley, in October. There were riders like the flamboyant Lewis sisters, Annette and Michelle, from Essex, the Heffernans, Robert Bevis, as well as another future national rider, Michael Mac. He was very tall on his 14.2hh pony, but rode so 'lightly' that he didn't look underhorsed. He went on to become chairman of British Show Jumping, but sadly died in his early fifties.

Horse and Hound copy was usually phoned over but occasionally it was put on the train from Tunbridge Wells Central at a cost of £1.81. For Young Entry, I would head for places like Bicton, in Devon, Harwood Hall and Mill Lodge, both in East Anglia and my favourite, Hickstead. The atmosphere, organisation and synchronisation there were superb not just for the Derby meeting but for every fixture including the annual inter-Schools competition. It was also the venue in 1974 of the first ever team chase, across Douglas Bunn's farmland away from his immaculate showgrounds. It was invitation only, held on Good Friday and televised by the BBC. It was not for the faint-hearted, with some enormous natural hedges, and I was part of the racing journalists' team along with John Oaksey, Brough Scott, Robin Gray and Brian McSharry. Unfortunately, my effort ended ignominiously at the second fence.

A show of a very different nature in 1981 was organised by a neighbour to us in Newlands Farm, and George was taken along on the lead rein on the little palomino pony called Goldie that he had been given. He finished fourth in the best pony and sixth in the ride and run, with me leading the pony and T running alongside holding George.

I had also met a family in Cornwall, sold them a super little horse called Master Charles for their son to show-jump, and then, when neither really gelled at this sport, they asked me to ride him in a Cornish point-to-point. He ran so well that I promptly bought him back. In later years, he became a regular in open team chases for Jo Jewell, sister of Quorn huntsman Michael Farrin.

Lambs were still being sold at the 'farm gate' as well as at Ashford Market, and I also had a few good NH rides. Things were not going too well at home, though, (not for the first time), and I pondered whether giving up racing might ease the tension. I mentioned this to a close family friend and he replied, "But Anne, we'd miss you." It was heart-warming and gave me the encouragement to continue.

I rode King's Rhapsody in a three-mile chase at Southwell, some eight years before it became an all-weather course. It was a long way from home and we and the horse were kindly put up by Dick and Pam Saunders who we knew through point-to-pointing. It was the following year that Dick won the Grand National on Grittar, at the age of 48 years the oldest winning rider in the history of the race.

That summer also saw me taking up the offer of some rides in the new sport of Arab racing, mostly on a very useful horse called Shadow Royal. There were only a few meetings, mostly round open farm fields, although one was at Larkhill point-to-point course; today, there are some thirty or so fixtures all held on full racecourses.

The following year, 1982, we bought Holcombe Rogus, a fine upstanding promising young horse who had been finishing in mid-division in large novice hurdle races at grade 1 tracks. He adapted to his new life well – training was interrupted for all of them by the heaviest December snowfall since 1874 – and when he won first time out at Charing I was, with Mister Tack's three under his belt, briefly leading rider in the country.

Holcombe Rogus, winning at the Ashford Valley, Charing, 1982. Photo Horse and Hound

When I rode Holcombe Rogus back there on Easter Saturday hopes were high. But for some reason my usual nerves didn't leave me once I had mounted. For the first and only time they were still with me circling down at the start. In the race, first one leader fell, followed by the next one, leaving me in the lead. When we, too, fell I hit the ground one last (racing) time and quit there and then. My nerve had gone.

It was Easter 1982 and I had lived for and loved every moment of my racing career.

Point-to-pointing was the love of my life. David Evatt behind.

Within weeks, sadly, my marriage was also over. George was just four years old. I felt as if the whole of my young adult life had disappeared out of the window. I also felt ten years younger. I doubted lambing would enter my life again, but I would never forget that first year nor, especially, the orphan lambs, but horses and writing would always be a part of me.

So, it was pick up the pieces, dust myself down and face daunting new challenges. A whole new phase of my life beckoned.

The End

EPILOGUE:

In May 2017, shortly before his 89th birthday, T died peacefully in Berkshire whence he had moved after sixty years or more in Kent, to be near George. Twice in those final few years T and I went off together to the Prix de l'Arc de Triomphe in Paris – who'd have thought it! Until his early eighties T had continued to keep at least a few sheep, and to the end he had a faithful collie, Dotty, by his side, his closest companion and best friend.

It was both intuitive and appropriate that our son, George, who was not yet born at the time of our snowy first lambing, chose *While Shepherds Watched Their Flocks By Night* as one of the hymns for his funeral, for all that it was July.

A few weeks later, on a visit to Sussex, I drove by Newlands Farm. There was no sign of our little old gamekeepers' cottage. In its place was a five-bedroomed, 4-bathroomed house with five reception rooms, underfloor heating, cinema, bar, 33foot games room and more besides. Outside, it had modernised garage and stabling, and the land that was left was the field around it and the three-acre strip of woodland, in which was laid an Olympic sized equestrian sand arena. Not a trace of our original cottage remained, either inside or out, not even the arched windows.

The new property had been on the market the previous year for £2.75 million.

* * *

Lightning Source UK Ltd.
Milton Keynes UK
UKHW022344150722
405923UK00004B/305